The Marriage of Figaro

The Marriage of Figaro

WOLFGANG AMADEUS MOZART
TEXT BY ROBERT LEVINE

BLACK DOG
& LEVENTHAL
PUBLISHERS
NEW YORK

The enclosed compact discs {P} 1977 by EMI Records.
Digital remastering {P} & © EMI Records Ltd.
Product of EMI-Capitol Special Markets, 1750 North Vine Street
Los Angeles, CA 90028

Libretto reproduced by courtesy of Angel/EMI Classics

Published by
Black Dog & Leventhal Publishers, Inc.
151 West 19th Street
New York, NY 10011

Distributed by
Workman Publishing Company
708 Broadway
New York, NY 10003

Designed by Alleycat Design, Inc.

Photo Research: Anne Burns Images

Manufactured in   Singapore

ISBN: 1-57912-065-2

h g f e d c b

FOREWORD

The Marriage of Figaro is the result of one of the greatest creative collaborations in history. Mozart's musical genius, da Ponte's skillful realism and Beaumarchais's courageously honest subject matter combine to create perhaps the most successful opera buffa of all time. *Figaro* takes us through a single 'mad day' in the Almaviva household; unique in its chaos but wonderfully typical in its players, their lives and their relationships with each other. The music is joyful and complex, the characters are endearing and real and the plotlines are boisterously entertaining: *Figaro's* success is well-deserved.

You will hear the entire opera on the two compact discs included on the inside front and back covers of this book. As you explore the text, you will discover the story behind the opera and its creation, the background of the composer, biographies of the principal singers and conductor and the opera's libretto, both in the original Italian and in an English translation. Special commentary has been included throughout the libretto to aid in your appreciation and highlight key moments in the action and score.

Enjoy this book and enjoy the music.

OTHER TITLES IN THE SERIES

Aida

Carmen

Cavalleria Rusticana & I Pagliacci

Il Trovatore

La Bohème

La Traviata

Madama Butterfly

Rigoletto

The Barber of Seville

The Magic Flute

Tosca

ABOUT THE AUTHOR

*R*obert Levine is a New York based music and travel writer whose work has appeared in dozens of newspapers and periodicals around the world. In addition to his being Senior Classical Music Advisor to Amazon.com, he contributes to *Stereophile, Fanfare, Opera News* and *BBC Music Magazine* and acts as advisor to a handful of European opera companies and artists.

ACKNOWLEDGEMENTS

The author would like to thank Paul Harrington for his help in preparing the manuscript.

WOLFGANG AMADEUS MOZART (1756-1791)
PAINTING BY MARTIN MEYTENS II (1695-1770)

The Marriage of Figaro

In 1785 Wolfgang Amadeus Mozart was the most sought-after composer in Vienna. *Die Entführung aus dem Serail (The Abduction from the Seraglio)*, the exotic opera he had written three years prior, had made him famous in Viennese society. Immediately after its premiere, he found himself invited regularly to perform for Emperor Joseph II, Count Esterhazy, the Court Counselor and lesser courtiers. Even the great Franz Joseph Haydn recognized his talent and sought out his company. Nevertheless, Mozart and his new wife, Constanze (they were married in 1782), found themselves under constant financial stress; his carousing, entertaining and gambling increased with his artistic successes. Certainly these problems were related to his immaturity—at 29, he had been independent of his father for only a short time. Mozart seems to have assumed his income would increase commensurate with his rising fame, but this was not happening at the rate he had expected. He needed to cement his place in Viennese music and his

young family's financial well-being.

Although this was the most fertile period in his career, Mozart had not written an opera since *Abduction*. Opera was the most significant art form in Vienna, and could make or break a composer's reputation. To achieve the stability his family needed, it was clear that he should assume one of the court's musical positions—but this goal could be achieved only through renown. Accordingly, despite the impressive number of instrumental compositions he wrote during this period, Mozart also sought a libretto with which to secure his standing.

Mozart had a very fine understanding of what made an opera great. He wrote to his father, "In an opera the poetry must perforce be the obedient daughter of the music"; he knew what people listened for, and knew that the words could make an opera magical, or they could sap the music of its meaning and appeal. He had learned this after spending his childhood (Mozart wrote his first opera when he was 12) composing music for librettos handed to him as *faits accomplis* by his teachers and patrons. As an adult he worked closely with his librettists on all the operas he composed; he claimed to have read, and tossed out, hundreds of librettos in search of those worthy of his composition.

Lorenzo da Ponte was the librettist with whom Mozart wrote three of his greatest operas, *Le Nozze di Figaro*, *Don Giovanni* and *Cosi Fan Tutte*, and he could not have found a more appropriate partner. If Mozart was a rascal, he was a well-heeled one; he was always a good son and husband. However, da Ponte was a true adventurer, the sort of "bad boy" Mozart could never be. Born to Jewish parents in the Venetian city of Ceneda in 1749, his birth name was Emmanuele Conegliano until he was 14, when his widower father decided to marry a Christian

JOSEPH II OF
AUSTRIA
(1741-1790),
KING OF GERMANY
1764-1790,
HOLY ROMAN
EMPEROR
1765-1790,
KING OF AUSTRIA,
1780-1790

and converted to Catholicism. All the children were baptized by the Bishop of Ceneda, who gave his own name, Lorenzo da Ponte, to Emmanuele, the eldest son.

The new Lorenzo went on to become an ordained priest and led a life of amorous adventure in Venice. (Remember, this was the Age of Reason, and priests could do that sort of thing.) Eventually he became a teacher of rhetoric at the University of Treviso, but was dismissed in 1776 for writing poems seen as seditious and defamatory. Da Ponte's dismissal from the University was just the beginning of his colorful journey. His libertine ways caught up with him following an affair with a married woman (which produced a child) and a stint as a violinist in a brothel; in 1779 he was banished from the state of Venice entirely. From Venice he went to Germany and Austria; in Vienna he was appointed poet to the Imperial Theater, and met Mozart.

Da Ponte lived in Vienna until 1791 but he fell out of favor with Emperor Leopold II, Joseph II's successor. After publishing some vituperative attacks upon the new Emperor, he found himself banished from Austria as well. He next landed in Paris, then London, working for a time as a theater impresario and bookseller, but his stay there was cut short by money problems and he eventually fled again—this time to New York. He survived there by taking up jobs as a grocer and a distiller, eventually becoming the first Pro-fessor of Italian at Columbia University, where he wrote his famous and controversial memoirs. He died at 89 in 1838, and is buried in the Roman Catholic cemetery on East 11th Street in New York City.

The Marriage of Figaro was a well known play by Pierre-Augustin Caron de Beaumarchais (1732-99) when Mozart discovered it in 1785. The son of a watchmaker, Beaumarchais was one of his century's more colorful figures. He gave harp lessons to the daughters of Louis XV, speculated in grandiose business schemes, spent several years tied up in one of the age's most scandalous lawsuits, acted as a secret agent for France during a period of exile in England, published the first complete edition of Voltaire's works, ran guns to the American revolutionaries and founded the French Society of Dramatic Authors.

As a "dramatic author," Beaumarchais wrote several plays, and two of his comedies gained immortality. The first of these, *Le Barbier de Séville (The Barber of Seville)*, was first produced in 1775. An immensely important work during its time, it ingeniously blended the tra-

THE COUNT BEGS FOR FORGIVENESS IN THE FINAL SCENE, METROPOLITAN OPERA, 1985

dition of Moliére and the figures from the classical Italian *commedia dell' arte*. The youthful lover (Count Almaviva) and the miserly, pompous old man (Doctor Bartolo) contend for the hand of Rosina, and the Barber (Figaro), through sheer ingenuity, enables the Count to win.

The social criticism floating behind the comedic elements of Le Barbier was seen even more clearly in its 1778 sequel. *Le Mariage de Figaro (The Marriage of Figaro)* was an even more daring play, one that would have serious social and political reverberations. In it, Beaumarchais showed that the Almaviva marriage was less than successful, and that Figaro (now the Count's valet) finds himself pitted in another battle of wits, this time with the Count himself.

Almaviva, being an "enlightened" ruler, has recently done away with the *droit de seigneur*, an ancient privilege of the aristocracy that allowed them first-night privileges with any of their servants who marry. After abolition of this ancient custom, however, the Count's eyes have fallen upon Susanna, his wife's maid and Figaro's fiancèe. Finding himself passionately enamored of her, he attempts to convince Susanna to sell him the "right" he so recently—and gallantly—gave up. Not only the servants stand against the Count; even the Countess is forced to seek their aid and side with them in their machinations. Eventually she and they win: Figaro and Susanna marry, the Count and Countess's marriage is renewed and order is restored. In *Le Barbier de Séville* Beaumarchais parodies contemporary social conventions and touches upon political matters; in *Figaro* he goes even further. While the Count tries, like so many aristocrats of the period, to be enlightened, he finds himself very much at odds with this enlightenment. The common people are shown to be not only smarter, but also ethically and morally superior. Any aristocrat seeing this play could not have missed the meanings behind the clever repartee: It questioned their very right to rule.

The Marriage of Figaro's criticism of its time's social and political order (just five years before the bloody French Revolution) ensured the play a rocky start; it faced stiff censorship from the beginning. It was not until 1784, after some of Louis XVI's courtiers saw a private production and convinced him to allow a public performance, that the play was seen by the general public. It immediately became one of the greatest successes of the French theater.

Of course, any cultural event so well-received in Paris would become the talk of Europe, and the play was soon translated and spread throughout the

continent. In early 1785, a Viennese theater troupe led by Emanuel Schikaneder (later to be the librettist of Mozart's *The Magic Flute*) began rehearsing a German language version. Not surprisingly, the Imperial Censor did not allow the planned performance, though he permitted the play to be published.

Mozart brought a copy of the play to da Ponte, who wrote in his memoirs that he turned it into a libretto in six weeks. Apparently he was not alone in either his inspiration or hard work, for da Ponte also reported that, "As fast as I wrote the words, Mozart set them to music." The rascality that the two seem to have shared enabled them to work as an impressive team. However, it was more than shared character traits with his librettist that inspired Mozart in composing *Figaro*, for there was much in the play with which he could identify. Figaro, like Mozart, was in constant conflict with his superiors. Just a few years earlier, Mozart had angrily rebelled and been (literally) booted out of the service of the Archbishop of Salzburg. Since then he had found himself competing with jealous men in superior positions who would stop at nothing to impede his progress.

Once the opera was completed, it was da Ponte who convinced the Emperor to allow it to be performed, but this was no simple matter. Joseph II was no fan of the original play, fearing its political implications, and both the Abbe Casti (da Ponte's chief rival) and Antonio Salieri (Mozart's chief rival), as well as the court's opera manager Count Orsini-Rosenberg, tried to prevent its production. (Salieri, Joseph II's court composer, was the most famous of Mozart's competitors. He recognized Mozart's superior talent, and acted whenever possible to ensure that his own position would not be endangered by the younger composer. Contrary to what was presented in the play and movie *Amadeus*, however, there is no evidence that Salieri was instrumental in Mozart's death.) Only after the Emperor was satisfied that the inflammatory scenes from the original play had been removed or rewritten, and that it had been turned into a harmless farce, did he give permission to perform *Figaro*.

The significance of *Figaro* was recognized at its premiere on May 1, 1786 at the court theater. Mozart conducted from the keyboard, and the audience's recep-

tion was generally favorable. The opera's popularity grew astoundingly with each repetition, and by the third performance it is said there were so many encores that in order to keep performances from running all night, the Emperor banned the repetition of ensemble pieces.

While this tale is certainly evidence of the public's feelings about the opera, written reviews from the time are equally telling. Not long after the premiere, a reviewer wrote in the *Wiener Realzeitung*:

"The public…did not really know on the first day where it stood. It heard many a bravo from unbiased connoisseurs, but obstreperous louts in the upper-most story exerted their hired lungs…to deafen singers alike with their ST! and Pst!; and consequently opinions were divided at the end of the piece…Apart from that, it is true that the first performance was none of the best owing to the difficulty of the composition. But now, after several performances, one would be subscribing either to the cabal or to tastelessness if one were to maintain that Herr Mozart's music is anything but a masterpiece of art."

Oddly, *Figaro* played for only nine days in Vienna. Why was its run so short? We do not know to what extent the machinations of Salieri or any of Mozart's other rivals might have been re-sponsible. One must not forget that despite da Ponte's editing (and in some way, perhaps, because of it) the social and political criticism contained within *Figaro* could not have pleased the powerful nobility who must have felt the sting that Mozart so artfully delivered.

In December 1786 *Figaro* was staged in Prague so successfully that Mozart traveled there in January 1787 to conduct a performance. He was clearly thrilled with Prague's acceptance of his work, as he wrote to a friend, "Here they talk about

ANTONIO SALIERI (1750-1825)

nothing but *Figaro*. Nothing is played, sung or whistled but *Figaro*. No opera is drawing like *Figaro*. Nothing, nothing but *Figaro*." The commission for a new opera (which would be *Don Giovanni*) that the company gave him further confirmed that Mozart had written a masterpiece.

From the beginning of Figaro, the music signals that we are about to hear an intense and complex story. Its overture is playful and conspiratorial, with an unmistakable tension. This manic tension, not unlike Warner Brothers's cartoon music of a century and a half later, prepares us for the madcap adventures we are about to witness; however, unlike with cartoon music, there is real sobriety behind the tomfoolery. Indeed, it might be said that this juxtaposition of cheerfulness and tension hammers home the seriousness of Figaro's themes. It presents us with an aural warning of larger issues at hand.

Figaro is very much more than lovely music. Unlike classical drama and classical opera, which is populated by gods and goddesses, Figaro is peopled with real characters and real issues that resound even for modern audiences. (Indeed, the 1980s saw opera director Peter Sellars update the action—successfully, intelligently and non-anachronistically—to today in New York's Trump Tower!) Beyond the political commentary in the opera, and perhaps even more important, was the theme of order in disordered times. This was, after all, the Age of Enlightenment, and the eve of a long and bloody revolution. Without doubt, Mozart sensed the political undercurrents, and one is therefore struck by the hopefulness behind even the saddest pieces in the opera; there is always a smile somewhere behind the tears. At the same time, deceit, another major theme, is used effectively only by characters who have no other recourse. The Count, for example, is a schemer, but he's not very good at it, and fails whenever he attempts to match wits with his servants. The servants and the Countess succeed in their intrigues simply because they

COSTUME SKETCH FOR
FIGARO AND SUSANNA,
18TH CENTURY
AUSTRIAN ENGRAVING

lack the Count's power. They have no other way to foil his plans. But it should also be noted that nobody in Figaro actually harms anyone else.

These are not one-dimensional characters. We see this even in the Count and Countess. Whether they emerge triumphant in the end or not, Mozart still re-served his most powerful musical portraits for the aristocracy. The Count is the villain of the piece—but not a cardboard, mustache-twirling one. In him we see a man coming to terms with his age. He represents order, power, stability (even if his actions seem to undermine everything he represents), and Mozart pokes plenty of fun at him. However, despite his buffoonery, the Count is realistic and frightening; these qualities lie just beneath the surface, and sometimes explode. For example, in the third act, after he overhears Susanna and Figaro plotting against him—actual evidence at last that he is being played for a fool—he express-es his outrage in a vicious (and very challenging vocally) recitative and aria, *"Vedro, mentr'io sospiro (Shall I live to see a servant of mine happy and enjoying pleasure, while I am left to sigh.…Only the hope of ven-geance…makes me rejoice)."* By using an instrumental technique combining small phrases which are different from each other but still linked, Mozart shows the Count's mounting rage and his frayed emotional state, culminating in a desire for revenge.

In the Countess we see a grace and dignity that is at times awe-inspiring. *The Barber of Seville* ended with her as the happy wife of Almaviva, but in *Figaro* she is an older, wearied woman. Her deep sadness and the decency with which she accepts it, while acting to "fix" things for herself, impresses us most. Her actions are an attempt to right a sinking ship. The Count no longer returns her affections and chases servant girls, yet leaving him is not an option—not only is it simply not done, but it also would only add to the disintegration taking place throughout the palace. As Countess she must solve these problems and return pro-

priety and enlightenment to her home. This is precisely what she does at the end of the opera, when the Count apologizes with a melody so simple and lovely that only a heart of stone would turn him down. But while the Countess is attempting to reestablish order in the palace, she has no choice but to turn to her maid, Susanna, for assistance.

The impact of the Countess's character is heightened by the fact that she does not appear until the second act. We know from Mozart's letters that this was an intentional ploy: Act One introduced us to the farce, but the Countess, who opens Act Two, must make us realize that there are real feelings involved as well. We meet her as she sings a plea for love, *"Porgi amor (Return my loved one to me, or let me die)"*, and a sobering influence sets in. As if to protect herself from her own sorrow, she goes along with Susanna's and Figaro's machinations. It diverts her; despite her station above her servants, she becomes one with them—she's empathetic and feels their predicament as well. But when she's alone her sadness, doubts and humiliation return. In her third act recitative, *"E Susanna non vien,"* she voices her embarrassment: *"To what shame am I reduced by a cruel husband?"* And in the aria which follows, *"Dove sono (Where are the happy moments of sweetness and pleasure?)"*, she wishes her constancy would change *"his ungrateful heart."* Despite this disgrace, she pushes on to fulfill her duties, yet this charming, sympathetic character still manages to enjoy herself. It is this underlying *joie de vivre* that makes the Countess, and Mozart unique and so exquisite.

FREDERICA VON STADE
AS CHERUBINO

THE OPERA HOUSE IN PRAGUE

But what of Figaro and Susanna? *"Cinque...dieci...venti,"* the opening piece of Act One, shows Figaro and Susanna preparing for their wedding day. He is innocently—but a little randily—measuring the room to see if the bed the Count has so generously given them will fit. She's trying on a hat—but abandons that to let him in on the Count's ulterior motives after calling the naïve Figaro a "dolt." Figaro is horrified—he believes that the Count has given them this bed and a room located strategically near his own out of kindness and to make Figaro's job easier. Susanna is the worldly one—she has no doubt that the Count wants her close so he can seduce her more conveniently.

Susanna's realism and insight is a recurring theme. She understands what occurs in the castle and has the Countess's ear—it is Susanna who hatches the plans that make up the witty complications in the plot. She never loses her dignity, and only once—briefly—misreads a situation: the moment after Figaro discovers that Marcellina is his mother, a twist that even Susanna could not have foreseen.

Once aware of the Count's intentions toward Susanna, Figaro angrily sings, *"Se vuol ballare (If, my dear Count, you feel like dancing, I'll play the tune on my little guitar)."* The aria changes tempo three times, moving from Figaro's sar-

casm to his righteous anger, to his refusal to allow the Count to bully him. "It shall not be: Figaro has said it," he concludes. He has reacted, but he has no way to solve the problem. (This task, as do most tasks, falls to Susanna.) And Figaro remains the same throughout the opera: He reacts. In the final act, when he thinks Susanna might be betraying him, he delivers a diatribe on the fickleness of women *("Aprite un po' quegli occhi")* in an aria which took the place of a tirade against the upper classes that appeared in the Beaumarchais origi-nal. Figaro remains likeable and sympa-thetic, yet again, his judgment is off.

Cherubino, the Count's page, is another pivotal character. Just coming into adolescence, this young man (always

FIGARO, IN AN ENGRAVING BY EMILE ANTOINE BAYARD (1837-1891)

played by a woman), even more than Figaro, is in opposition to the Count. He is in love with the Countess (and every other woman in the palace, for that matter), and the lonely Countess cannot help but be charmed by his attentions. But he bunglingly shows up at all the wrong times, and can't seem to help reminding the Count of the aging process and the fact that the Count is vainly attempting to hang onto his youth by pursuing every available beauty. This young punk continually reveals the Count's unraveling dignity. The Count exiles him (often) and the others ridicule him, but it's impossible not to like him, so ardent and unprotected are his feelings, as exhibited by his breathless, panting first-act aria and almost embarrassingly sincere second-act aria.

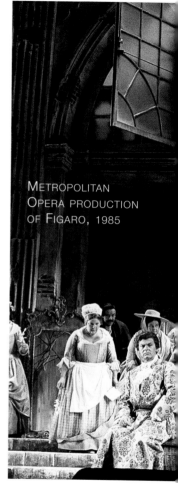

METROPOLITAN OPERA PRODUCTION OF FIGARO, 1985

If *Figaro* is a musical masterpiece, as well as a masterpiece of social satire, its politics, no less masterful in a subtle presentation, did not help Mozart further his career. Its initial popularity in Vienna did not stop the production's run from ending quite abruptly. And though the fervor with which it was accepted in Prague led to more operatic commissions for him, even these successes did not have the required effect for Mozart. The most important, lucrative commissions and audiences were in Vienna.

Even today one can't help but be struck by this vital and overwhelmingly

rich work. In *Figaro*, Mozart does more than write brilliant music to a wonderful libretto; he creates a vibrant story that contemporary audiences can still compre-

Celebrating 10 Seasons of The Metropolitan Opera on TV
Mozart's "Le Nozze di Figaro"
Wednesday, April 23
8 PM (EST) on PBS

With Carol Vaness, Kathleen Battle,
Frederica von Stade. Ruggero Raimondi
and Thomas Allen. James Levine conducts.
Telecast hosted by Joanne Woodward.
Simulcast in Stereo FM in many cities.
With English subtitles

Mozart matches a sense of humor with a sense of humanity in Jean-Pierre Ponnelle's lively new production of "The Marriage of Figaro." It seems a comedy of manners, morals and machinations as "Figaro" and his intended bride, Susanna, match wits with the autocratic power of Count Almaviva and his Court. But this delightful evening of mixups, mistaken identities and misunderstandings leads to a joyous finale that's as moving as it is amusing.

TEXACO PHILANTHROPIC FOUNDATION INC.

Funding for "Live From The Met" is made possible by a major grant from Texaco Philanthropic Foundation Inc. with additional grants from ⓟ PIONEER® Electronic Corporation, the National Endowment for the Arts, the Corporation for Public Broadcasting, and the Charles E. Culpeper Foundation.

CELEBRATED ARTIST AL HIRSCHFELD'S RENDERING OF THE 1986 CAST OF FIGARO, IN AN ADVERTISEMENT FOR A TELEVISED PRODUCTION.

hend. How many men going through a mid-life crisis might understand the Count's issues and feel his rising rage, so palpable in the music? Certainly the predicament—and the sadness—of the Countess is not unknown to wives (and husbands, for that matter) today. How many young couples might recognize the challenges Figaro and Susanna face in learning to trust one another? And Cherubino? Well, most of us remember what it was like to be an adolescent coming to terms with sexuality and its resulting challenges and awkwardness.

The political message that seems to have limited Mozart's financial and professional success during his lifetime was quickly overcome with the passage of a few years, yet the compelling and sensitive characterizations in this work remain to keep *The Marriage of Figaro* relevant to modern ears. More than two centuries after its premiere, audiences still clamor for its outrageousness, it truths, its slapstick, its tears and its message of forgiveness.

The Story of the Opera

ACT I

The curtain rises on the wedding day of Count Almaviva's valet, Figaro, and the Countess's maid, Susanna. We see Figaro and Susanna in a sparsely furnished room in the Count's palace, Aguafrescas, near Seville. Figaro is measuring the space for their connubial bed, but when Susanna learns that this room is to be theirs, she warns him that the location is unwise because of the Count's designs on her. Figaro, astonished and furious, determines to thwart his master's aims.

They leave and Dr. Bartolo and Marcellina, the Count's middle-aged housekeeper, enter. She tells Bartolo that Figaro owes her money, and has promised to marry her if he cannot pay off the debt. Bartolo rejoices at the idea of forcing Figaro to marry this older woman, rather than the youthful and beautiful, Susanna. He harbors old hostility toward Figaro, and sees a glimmer of potential revenge. As Marcellina is leaving, Susanna enters and there is a brief but acrimonious encounter between these rivals. Next the Count's page, Cherubino, enters and tells Susanna he is to be sent into exile, as yesterday the Count caught him with Barbarina, the daughter of the gardener, Antonio. Cherubino tells Susanna he does not want to leave, for he is in love with the Countess (and the rest of womankind). Before he can leave, Cherubino spies the Count approaching and dives behind a nearby chair. The Count, entering, begins to tell Susanna of his desire for her, but not long into his impassioned speech they hear Don Basilio's voice; now the Count hides behind the chair as Cherubino deftly slips around to sit in it, covered by a lady's robe. Basilio, Susanna's music teacher and the Count's factotum, tells her how Cherubino adores the Countess; this infuriates the jealous Count, who comes out of hiding. He relates his recent discovery of Cherubino at Barbarina's, and while doing so un-covers the page once more in a lady's chamber.

Figaro enters with a group of peasants who sing the Count's praises for recently abolishing the *droit du seigneur*. Figaro asks the Count to place a white, virginal headdress on Susanna's head and give her away in marriage, but the Count avoids the issue by postponing the ceremony with a "generous" offer of a lavish party in their honor later in the day. The peasants leave and the Count punishes Cherubino by ordering him to take a commission and foreign posting in his own regiment. Figaro lightheartedly warns the nervous young officer about the rigors of military life.

ACT II

In her chamber, the Countess mourns the fading of her husband's love. Susanna enters, then Figaro. Figaro tells the Countess he has hatched a plot to distract the Count from Susanna. He has had a note delivered to the Count saying that the Countess has an assignation that evening with a lover; he also has Susanna invite the Count to meet her, and plans to send Cherubino, disguised as Susanna, in her place to the assignation. Figaro leaves and Cherubino arrives. He sings a love song he has written, then Susanna playfully begins to dress him as a woman. She rushes off to find a piece of ribbon, and he is in his shirtsleeves with the Countess when the Count knocks on the door. Cherubino hides in the dressing room, but upon entering the jealous, suspicious Count senses his wife's confusion. The combination of Figaro's note and her uncharacteristically locked door convinces him that she has a lover within. When there is a noise from the dressing room, the Countess tells the Count that it is only Susanna, and refuses to give him the key to check the room for himself. The Count decides to go get tools to break down the door, taking his wife with him and locking the door from the outside.

Susanna, who was in her own room and had entered unnoticed during the argument, tells Cherubino he may safely come out; he escapes by jumping out the window. She takes his place in the dressing room and re-locks door. Upon the couple's return, the Countess admits that it is a partly dressed Cherubino in the dressing room. As the enraged Count, his sword drawn, approaches the door, Susanna demurely steps out; the Count can only apologize to his equally nonplussed wife.

Now Figaro enters with news that the musicians have assembled for the wedding. The Count questions him about the letter he received earlier, having just learned from the Countess and Susanna that Figaro was its author. Figaro denies knowledge of it, and Antonio bursts into the room: Some of his prize plants have been destroyed by someone leaping from the window in this chamber. Figaro, who knows the situation, says that it was he who jumped from the window. Antonio goes to hand him a paper dropped near the broken pots, but the Count intercepts it. He questions Figaro about it; fortunately the Countess recognizes the paper as

Cherubino's commission and is able to furtively inform Figaro of this fact. He explains that he had the paper because (after being prompted again by the Countess) it needs the Count's seal. Marcellina, Bartolo and Basilio now enter and demand justice for Marcellina, ending the act in a complete muddle.

ACT III

In the main hall, the Count reflects on the situation. Susanna enters and tells him she is willing to comply with his desires. She plans to use the dowry he had promised her in return for her compliance to pay off Figaro's debt to Marcellina. As she leaves, the Count overhears her passing remark to Figaro, "Our case is won." Realizing that he is being tricked, and furious to think that his servant may enjoy what he cannot, the Count, is left to stew.

Figaro, Marcellina, Dr. Bartolo and Don Basilio meet with the Count who, as lord of the land, rules on the advice of the lawyer Don Curzio that Figaro must pay Marcellina or marry her. But now, to everyone's amazement, the story unfolds that Figaro is a foundling—he is Marcellina's long-lost son (not the son of a nobleman, as he had thought)—and his father is none other than Dr. Bartolo. Just as Figaro embraces his newly discovered mother, Susanna enters. Her initial anger and confusion turns to happiness when she learns what has transpired. The Count, meanwhile, is once more frustrated, learning of the true situation. Thereupon Marcellina and Bartolo decide to make that evening's festivities into a double wedding.

The Count departs; Cherubino and Barbarina pass through the hall, talking of the plan to dress him as a girl. The Countess, alone in her chamber, laments her lost happiness and the stratagem to which she is reduced in the hope of regaining her husband.

Next, in the Countess's chamber, the Countess and Susanna continue the plot to catch the Count and end his philandering. The Countess dictates a letter to Susanna—to be signed by Susanna—setting up a rendezvous. They seal it with a pin, to be returned in acknowledgment. A group of peasant girls, led by Barbarina, come to bring flowers to the Countess. Cherubino, disguised as a girl, is amongst them, but is revealed by Antonio, who enters with the Count. The Count's anger is quickly diverted when Barbarina reminds him that he has promised her a favor in return for her affections, and she claims Cherubino as that favor.

Entering, Figaro urges that the party and dancing begin. A march is heard as peasants enter, sing once again in praise of the enlightened Count, and dance a fandango. The marriage ceremony follows, during which Susanna surreptitiously slips her note to the Count. Although Figaro did not see her hand it to him, he notes that the Count has apparently pricked his finger on a sealing pin while opening a love letter. Finally, the Count promises a fabulous party that evening to celebrate the weddings.

ACT IV

We find Barbarina in the garden looking for the pin the Count had given her to return to Susanna; she has dropped it. Figaro enters and she tells him she has lost the pin the Count asked her to bring to Susanna. Not knowing about this plot, Figaro assumes the worst. He tells Marcellina, who runs to warn Susanna. Meanwhile, Figaro assembles Bartolo, Basilio and most of the other characters to hide in the garden and help him uncover his new wife's infidelity. He conceals himself as Susanna and the Countess enter. They have exchanged clothes, and Susanna, having spotted Figaro hiding, sings raptly but ambiguously of her approaching bliss. Figaro, his suspicious mind reeling, bursts with an impassioned rant about woman's infidelity.

The Countess, disguised as Susanna, awaits the Count. But Cherubino stumbles once more upon the proceedings and makes a pass at her; that ends abruptly when the Count enters. The Count leads "Susanna" to an arbor, but hearing Figaro pass by noisily, goes to hide himself. Figaro spots the "Countess" (Susanna in costume) and tells her that the Count is with Susanna. Susanna forgets to conceal her voice, Figaro recognizes her and at last realizes what is going on. Unable to resist teasing her, he pleads passionate love to the "Countess". Not seeing through Figaro's game, Susanna punches him. Figaro quickly explains that he knew it was she, and the reconciled pair continue the charade for the returning Count. The Count, enraged at discovering Figaro and a woman he thinks is the Countess making love, summons everyone to witness his wife's betrayal. Everyone begs him to forgive her, but he is adamant—until he hears the true Countess's voice join the crowd. He immediately realizes what he has done, and kneels to beg her forgiveness; she cannot withhold it. As the opera ends, all joyfully "hasten to the revelry" that the Count had earlier promised.

The Marriage of Figaro

WOLFGANG AMADEUS MOZART (1756-1791)

Dietrich Fischer-Dieskau..Count Almaviva
Heather Harper...Countess Almaviva
Judith Blegen...Susanna
Geraint Evans..Figaro
Teresa Berganza...Cherubino
Birgit Finnilä...Marcellina

Daniel Barenboim—Conductor, English Chamber Orchestra

The Performers

Dietrich Fischer-Dieskau (Count Almaviva)

Acknowledged as one of the great baritones of the 20th century, Fischer-Dieskau was born in Berlin in 1925 to a self-taught musician father and an amateur pianist mother. His musical education began with piano lessons at the age of 9 and voice at 16. In 1942-43, he continued his voice study with Hermann Weissenborn at the Berlin Musikhochschule. Drafted into the army in 1943, he was captured by the Americans while serving in Italy in 1945. He returned to Germany after his release in 1947, and made his first professional appearance as a soloist in the Brahms *Deutschen Requiem* in Badenweiler. He resumed his study with Weissenborn in Berlin and performed on radio broadcasts during this time. In 1948 he made his operatic debut in the bass role of Colas in a broadcast of Mozart's youthful opera *Bastien und Bastienne*. His debuted on stage a few months later as Rodrigue, Marquis of Posa in Verdi's *Don Carlos* at the Berlin Städtische Opera, where he remained an in-valuable member for 35 years.

Although Fischer-Dieskau continued to pursue his operatic career at leading opera houses and festivals in Europe, it was as a *lieder* and concert artist that he became world-famous. In 1955 he made his American debut with the Cincin-

DIETRICH FISCHER-DIESKAU (COUNT ALMAVIVA)
AND KIRI TE KANAWA (COUNTESS ALMAVIVA), 1984

nati Symphony Orchestra, and soon after his recital debut at New York's Town Hall. His best—known operatic roles included Count Almaviva, Don Giovanni, Papageno, Macbeth, Falstaff, Hans Sachs, Mandryka and Wozzeck. He created the role of Gregor Mittenhofer in Henze's *Elegy for Young Lovers* (1961) and the title role in Reimann's *Lear*. Among the honors he received were membership in the Berlin Akademie der Künste (1956), the Mozart Medal of Vienna (1962), Kammersanger of Berlin (1963), the Grand Cross of Merit of the Federal Republic of Germany (1978), honorary doctorates from Oxford University (1978) and the Sorbonne in Paris (1980) and the Gold Medal of the Royal Philharmonic Society of London (1988).

HEATHER HARPER (Countess Almaviva)

The distinguished Irish soprano Heather Harper was born in Belfast in 1930. While studying at Trinity College of Music in London, she also took voice lessons with Helene Isepp and Frederic Husler. In 1954 she debuted as Lady Macbeth with the Oxford University Opera Club. She joined the English Opera Group (1956-75); performed for the first time at the Glyndebourne Festival in 1957, at Covent Garden as Helena in *A Midsummer Night's Dream* in 1962 and at the Bayreuth Festival as Elsa in 1967. In 1969 she sang in the United States and South America. Her final public appearance as a singer was in 1990.

Some of Harper's best-known roles included Arabella, Marguerite, Gutrune, Hecuba, Anne Trulove in *The Rake's Progress*, The Woman in *Erwartung*, Ellen Orford in *Peter Grimes* and the role of Nadia in Tippett's *The Ice Break* (1977), which she created. She later became a professor at the Royal College of Music in London and director of singing studies at the Britten-Pears School. In 1965, Harper was made a Commander of the British Empire.

JUDITH BLEGEN (Susanna)

Judith Blegen was born in Missoula, Montana in 1941. She studied violin and singing at the Curtis Institute of Music in Philadelphia (1959-64). After studying with Luigi Ricci in Italy, she sang at the Nuremberg Opera from 1964 to 1966. Her American debut was at the Santa Fe Festival in 1969, as Emily in Menotti's satirical opera *Help, Help, the Globolinks!*, written especially for her. In 1970, Blegen debuted at the Metropolitan Opera as Papagena in *Die Zauberflöte;* her light, silvery soprano found an ideal home in Mozart's operas. She continued to appear at the Met in a variety of roles, debuted at the Paris Opéra in 1977, and sang at several other European opera houses as well.

JUDITH BLEGEN AS SUSANNA, 1975

GERAINT EVANS (Figaro)

Sir Geraint Evans was a world-famous baritone from Cilfynydd, Wales, born in 1922. He began voice study in Cardiff at the age of 17, but World War II interrupted his education. After serving in the RAF he resumed his studies in Hamburg with Theo Hermann, then studied with Fernando Carpi in Geneva and Walter Hyde at the Guildhall School of Music in London. His operatic debut was as the Nightwatchman in *Die Meistersinger von Nürnberg* at Covent Garden in London (1948), where he became a leading member of the company. From 1960 through 1961 he sang at the Glyndebourne Festival; his first United States appearance was with the San Francisco Opera. He debuted at Milan's La Scala (1960), the Vienna State Opera (1961), the Salzburg Festival (1962), the Metropolitan Opera (1964) and the Paris Opéra (1975). His best-known roles include Figaro, Leporello, Papageno, Beckmesser, Falstaff, Don Pasquale and Wozzeck. In 1984 he gave his final opera performance, as Dulcamara, at Covent Garden. For his notable performances and his work as an opera producer, Evans was made a Commander of the British Empire in 1959, and in 1969 he was knighted.

TERESA BERGANZA (Cherubino)
Mezzo-soprano Teresa Berganza was born in Madrid in 1935. She studied at the Madrid Conservatory, and sang at the Florence May Festival and Aix-en-Provence in 1957. The next year she made her United States debut (in Dallas), as well as at the Glyndebourne Festival and in 1960 sang at Covent Garden in London. Cherubino was the role in which she debuted at the Metropolitan Opera. Berganza was an admired Rosina (*Il Barbiere di Siviglia*), Carmen, Dorabella (*Cosi Fan Tutte*) and Zerlina (*Don Giovanni*).

TERESA BERGANZA, 1993

BIRGIT FINNILÄ (Marcellina)
This Swedish contralto was born in Falkenberg in 1931. She studied voice in Göteborg and with Roy Henderson at the Royal Academy of Music in London. Since her 1963 concert debut in Göteborg, she has performed with major European, American, Australian and Israeli orchestras.

DANIEL BARENBOIM (Conductor, English Chamber Orchestra)
Born in Buenos Aires, Argentina in 1942, this talented pianist and conductor began his musical education with his parents. His first public performance (at the piano) was in Buenos Aires when he was seven years old. In 1952 the Barenboims settled in Israel, and during the summers of 1954 and 1955 he studied piano in Salzburg with Edwin Fischer and conducting under Igor Markevitch. From 1954 to 1956 he studied music theory with Nadia Boulanger in Paris and enrolled at the Accademia di Santa Cecilia in Rome, where in 1956 he became one of the youngest students ever to receive a diploma. During this period he also studied conducting with Carlo Zecchi at the Accademia Musicale Chigiana in Siena. After giving recitals in Paris (1955) and London (1956), he made his American debut at Carnegie Hall in New York, performing Prokofiev's First Piano Concerto with Leopold Stokowski.

Barenboim's debut as a conductor occurred in Haifa in 1957. Ten years later he led the Israel Philharmonic on its tour of the United States, and a year after that he conducted the London Symphonic Orchestra in New York. Barenboim's debut as an opera conductor was at the Edinburgh Festival in 1972. In 1975 he was named music director of the Orchestre de Paris. Barenboim was named artistic director of the new Bastille Opera in Paris. In 1988 , but after a headline-making falling out with the French Minister of Culture he left (in 1989) to succeed Sir Georg Solti as music director of the Chicago Symphony Orchestra, a post he still holds. He is also the General Music Director of the Deutsche Staatsoper Berlin.

The Libretto

OVERTURE

disc no. 1/track 1 *No. 1: Duettino*

Count Almaviva's Castle near Seville. (A half-furnished room with a large arm-chair in the centre. Figaro is measuring the floor. Susanna is trying on a hat in front of a mirror.)

FIGARO
Cinque...dieci...venti...Trenta...tentasei...quarantatre...

SUSANNA
Ora sì. ch'io son contenta, Sembra fatto inver per me.

FIGARO
Cinque...

SUSANNA
Guarda un po', mio caro Figaro.

FIGARO
dieci...

SUSANNA
guarda un po' mio caro Figaro...

FIGARO
venti...

FIGARO
Five...ten...twenty...thirty...thirty-six...forty-three...

SUSANNA
How happy I am now you'd think it had been made for me.

FIGARO
Five...

SUSANNA
Look a moment, dearest Figaro.

FIGARO
ten...

SUSANNA
look a moment, dearest Figaro.

FIGARO
twenty...

SUSANNA
guarda un po',

FIGARO
trenta...

SUSANNA
guarda un po', guarda adesso il mio cappello!

FIGARO
trentasei...

SUSANNA
guarda adesso il mio cappello.

FIGARO
quarantatre...

SUSANNA
guarda un po', mio caro Figaro, ecc.

FIGARO
Sì, mio core. or è più bello, sembra fatto
inver per te.

SUSANNA
Guarda un po', ecc.

FIGARO
Sì, mio core, ecc.

SUSANNA
Ora sì ch'io son contenta, ecc.

FIGARO
Sì, mio core, ecc.

SUSANNA
look a moment.

FIGARO
thirty...

SUSANNA
look a moment, look here at my cap!

FIGARO
thirty-six...

SUSANNA
look here at my cap.

FIGARO
forty-three...

SUSANNA
look a moment, etc.

FIGARO
Yes, dear heart, it's better that way; you'd
think it had been made for you.

SUSANNA
Look a moment, etc.

FIGARO
Yes, dear heart, etc.

SUSANNA
How happy I am now, etc.

FIGARO
Yes, dear heart, etc.

SUSANNA, FIGARO
Ah il mattino alle nozze vicino,

SUSANNA
quant'è dolce a l mio tenero sposo,

FIGARO
quant'è dolce al tuo tenero sposo,

SUSANNA, FIGARO
questo cappellino vezzoso, che Susanna ella stessa si fe', ecc.

Recitativo

SUSANNA
Cosa stai misurando, caro il mio Figaretto?

FIGARO
Io guardo se quel letto, che ci destina il Conte, farà buona figura in questo loco.

SUSANNA
In questa stanza?

FIGARO
Certo, a noi la cede generoso il padrone.

SUSANNA
Io per me te la dono.

FIGARO
E la ragione?

SUSANNA *(Sì tocca la fronte)*
La ragione l'ho qui.

SUSANNA, FIGARO
Ah, with our wedding day so near...

SUSANNA
how pleasing to my gentle husband.

FIGARO
how pleasing to your gentle husband.

SUSANNA, FIGARO
is this charming little cap which Susanna made herself! etc.

SUSANNA
What are you measuring, you dear little Figaro?

FIGARO
I want to know whether the bed which the Count is giving us will look good in this spot.

SUSANNA
In this room?

FIGARO
Certainly, this one was granted us by our generous patron.

SUSANNA
Then I turn it over to you.

FIGARO
Your reason?

SUSANNA *(tapping her forehead)*
The reason is up here.

FIGARO
Perché non puoi far, che passi un po' qui?

SUSANNA
Perché non voglio; sei mio servo, o no?

FIGARO
Ma non capisco perché tanto ti spiace la
più comoda stanza palazzo.

SUSANNA
Perché io son la Susanna, e sei pazzo.

FIGARO
Grazie; non tanti elogi, guarda un poco, se
potria sì meglio star in altro loco.

No. 2 Duettino

FIGARO
Se a caso Madama la notte ti chiama,
dindin, in due passi da quella puoi gir.
Vien poi l'occasione che vuolmi il padrone,
dondon, in tre salti lo vado a servir.

SUSANNA
Così se il mattino il caro contino, dindin, e
ti manda tre miglia lontan, dindin, dondon, a mia porta il diavol lo porta, ed ecco
in tre salti...

FIGARO
Susanna, pian pian, ecc.

FIGARO
Why can't you let it out for a moment?

SUSANNA
Because I don't wish to. Are you my humble servant or not?

FIGARO
I don't understand why you are so dis-
pleased with the most comfortable room in
the palace.

SUSANNA
Because I am Susanna, and you are insane.

FIGARO
Thank you, spare the compliments; but
consider whether any other place would be
better.

FIGARO
If perchance Madame should call you at
night, ding ding: in two steps from here
you'd be there. And then when the time
comes my master wants me, dong dong: in
three bounds I am ready to serve him.

SUSANNA
Likewise some morning the dear little
Count, ding ding: may send you some
three miles away, ding, ding, dong dong:
the devil may send him to my door, and
behold, in three bounds...

FIGARO
Susanna, hush, hush, etc.

SUSANNA

ed ecco, in tre salti...dindin...dondon...
Ascolta!

FIGARO

Fa presto!

SUSANNA

Se udir brami il resto, discaccia i sospetti,
che torto mi fan.

FIGARO

Udir bramo il resto, i dubbi, i sospetti
gelare mi fan.

Recitativo

SUSANNA

Or bene; ascolta e taci.

FIGARO

Parla, che c'è di nuovo?

SUSANNA

Il signor Conte, stanco d'andar cacciando
straniere bellezze forestiere, vuole ancor nel
castello ritentar la sua sorte; né già di sua
consorte, bada bene, l'appetito gli viene.

FIGARO

E di chi dunque?

SUSANNA

Della tua Susannetta.

SUSANNA

and behold, in three bounds...ding, ding...
Listen!

FIGARO

Quickly!

SUSANNA

If you want to hear the rest, drop those suspicions that do me such wrong.

FIGARO

I will hear the rest; dubious suspicions
make my spine shiver.

SUSANNA

Then listen, and be quite.

FIGARO

Speak, what's the news?

SUSANNA

My lord, the Count, tired of going hunting
for new beauties in the country, wishes to
try his luck once more in the castle; nor is
it for the Countess, mind you, that his
appetite moves him.

FIGARO

For whom, then?

SUSANNA

For your little Susanna.

FIGARO
Di te?

SUSANNA
Di me medesma, ed ha speranza ch'al nobil suo progetto utilissima sia tal vicinanza.

FIGARO
Bravo! Tiriamo avanti.

SUSANNA
Queste grazie son, questa la cura ch'egli prende di te, della tua sposa.

FIGARO
Oh guarda un po', che carità pelosa!

SUSANNA
Chetati, or viene il meglio: Don Basilio, mio maestro di canto, e suo mezzano, nel darmi la lezione, mi ripete ogni dì questa canzone.

FIGARO
Chi! Basilio! Oh birbante!

SUSANNA
E credevi che fosse la mia dote merto de tuo be muso?

FIGARO
Me n'era lusingato.

SUSANNA
la destina per ottenere da me certe mezz'ore che il diritto feudale...

FIGARO
For you?

SUSANNA
For none other, and he hopes that for his noble endeavor our proximity will be most useful.

FIGARO
Marvelous! Go on.

SUSANNA
Hence his favours, hence the solicitous attentions he pays you, and your bride.

FIGARO
Oh, look out for his easy-going charity!

SUSANNA
Hush, now comes the best part: Don Basilio, my singing teacher and his go-between, when he gives me my lesson, every day repeats for him the same old tune.

FIGARO
Who! Basilio? Oh, the rogue!

SUSANNA
And you thought that he gave me my dowry to reward your good service?

FIGARO
So I flattered myself.

SUSANNA
It is intended to obtain from me certain favours that the lord of the manor...

FIGARO

Come! Ne' feudi suoi non l'ha il Conte
abolito?

SUSANNA

Ebben, ora è pentito, è par che tenti riscot-
tarlo da me.

FIGARO

Bravo! Mi piace! Che caro signor Conte! ci
vogliam divertir, trovato avete... Chi suona?
La Contessa.

SUSANNA

Addio, addio, addio, Figaro bello.

FIGARO

Coraggio, mio tesoro.

SUSANNA

E cervello.

FIGARO

What! Hasn't the Count abolished such
rights in his lands?

SUSANNA

Perhaps, but he's changed his mind and
wants to get them back from me.

FIGARO

Admirable! So be it: my beloved lord and master! We are at the mercy of your whim! You
have found...Who is ringing? The Countess.

SUSANNA

Farewell, farewell, my handsome Figaro.

FIGARO

Courage, my treasure.

SUSANNA

Keep your wits about you.

(she goes off)

disc no. 1/track 4   *No. 3: Cavatina* Having been told by his bride-to-be, Susanna, that his
employer, the Count, has designs on her, Figaro sings a mockingly courtly ballad
to him: The rhythms are easy-going but the text is bitter and provoking, and
Figaro practically speaks the words, some quietly, some at the top of his voice.
Despite the defiant message, Mozart keeps the mood light—the plucked strings
which "imitate" the guitar Figaro would play for the Count to dance to are
charming—plain and simple. Here is the character of Figaro in a nutshell—react-
ing quickly, far from subservient, witty—and angry with the situation he has
found himself in.

FIGARO

Bravo, signor padrone! Ora incomincio a
capir il mistero, e a veder schietto tutto il

FIGARO

Bravo, my lord! Now I begin to understand
the mystery, to see plainly your entire pro-

vostro progetto: a Londra, è vero? Voi ministro, io corriero, e la Susanna segreta ambasciatrice, non sarà, non sarà! Figaro il dice!

Se vuol ballare, signor contino, il chitarrino suonerò, sì, se vuol venire nella mia scuola, la capriola insegnerò, sì. Saprò, saprò, ma piano, meglio ogni arcano dissimulando scoprir potrò. L'arte schermendo, l'arte adoprando, di qua pungendo, di là scherzando, tutte macchine rovescierò. Se vuol ballare, ecc.

(he leaves. Bartolo and Marcellina enter, she with a contract in her hand)

Recitativo

BARTOLO
Ed aspettaste il giorno fissato per nozze a parlarmi di questo?

MARCELLINA
Io non mi perdo, dottor mio, di coraggio per romper de' sponsali più avanzati di questo bastò spesso un pretesto; ed egli ha meco, oltre questo contratto, certi impegni...so io...basta...conviene la Susanna atterrir, convien con arte impuntigliarla a rifiutare il Conte; egli per vendicarsi prenderà il mio partito, e Figaro così fia mio marito.

BARTOLO *(prende il contratto)*
Bene, io tutto farò; senza riserve tutto a me palesate.

ject: to London, is it? You the minister, I the courier, and Susanna secret ambassadress. It shall not be! Figaro speaks!

If you would dance, my pretty Count, I'll play the tune on my little guitar. If you will come to my dancing school I'll gladly teach you the capriole. You will learn quickly every dark secret, you will find out how to dissemble. The art of stinging, the art of conniving, fighting with this one, playing with that one, all of your schemes I'll turn inside out. If you would dance, etc.

BARTOLO
And you waited until this day appointed for the wedding to tell me this?

MARCELLINA
Not yet, my dear Doctor, have I lost hope; to break off marriages nearer completion than this one needs only a pretext, and that I have here, and, besides this contract, definite promises. I know...but enough! Now is the time to harass Susanna; we must contrive an imbroglio with the Count. He, to get revenge, will take my side and Figaro will thus become my husband.

BARTOLO *(taking the contract)*
Excellent. I shall do everything: keep me well posted.

(aside)

Avrei pur gusto di dare in moglie la mia
serva antica a chi mi fece un dì rapir l'amica.

I shall be only too glad to marry off my old
servant to the man who once ruined my
chances with Rosina.

No 4: Aria

La vendetta, oh, la vendetta, è un piacer
serbato ai saggi, l'obliar l'onte, gli oltraggi,
è bassezza, è ognor viltà. Coll'astuzio...
Coll'arguzia, col giudizio, col criterio..sì
potrebbe...il fatto è serio, ma credete sì
farà. Se tutto il codice dovessi volgere, se
tutto l'indice dovessi leggere, con un equiv-
oco, con un sinonimo, qualche garbuglio sì
troverà. Se tutto il codice, ecc. Tutta
Siviglia conosce Bartolo, il birbo Figaro
vinto sarà, ecc.

Revenge, oh, sweet revenge is a pleasure
reserved for the wise; to forgo shame, bold
outrage, is base and utter meanness. With
astuteness, with cleverness, with discretion,
with judgment if possible. The matter is
serious; but, believe me, it shall be done. If
I have to pore over the law books, if I have
to read all the extracts, with misunderstandings, with hocus-pocus he'll find himself in a turmoil. If I have to pore over, etc.
All Seville knows Bartolo, the scoundrel
Figaro shall be overcome!

(he goes)

Recitativo

MARCELLINA
Tutto ancor non ho perso: mi resta la speranza. Ma Susanna sì avanza, io vo' provar-
mi...fingiam di non vederla. E qualla
buona perla la vorrebbe sposar!

MARCELLINA
I haven't been stopped yet: my hopes are
very good. Ah, Susanna is coming: we'll
see. I'll pretend not to notice her. And this
is the bright pearl whom he's going to wed!

(enter Susanna)

SUSANNA
Di me favella.

SUSANNA
She's chattering about me.

MARCELLINA
Ma da Figaro alfine non può meglio sperar-si: l'argent fait tout.

SUSANNA
Che lingua! Manco male, ch'ognun sa quanto vale.

MARCELLINA
Brava! Questo è giudizio! Con quegli occhi modesti, con quell'aria pietosa, e poi...

SUSANNA
(Meglio è partir!)

MARCELLINA
(Che cara sposa!)

MARCELLINA
But I suppose she couldn't do better than Figaro. L'argent fait tout.

SUSANNA
(What a tongue!) It takes troubles to bring out a person's character.

MARCELLINA
Splendid! Here's justice! With those modest eyes! With that pious air, and still...

SUSANNA
(Now's the time to leave.)

MARCELLINA
(A pretty little wife!)

(They both want to leave and meet at the door)

disc no. 1/track 6   *no. 5: Duettino*   This tells us all we have to know about the relationship between Marcellina and Susanna—they hate each other. In two minutes Mozart gives us a portrait of one of the supremely bitchy relationships in opera.

(fa una riverenza)
Via, resti, servita, madama brillante.

SUSANNA *(fa una riverenza)*
Non sono sì ardita, madama piccante.

MARCELLINA *(fa una riverenza)*
No, prima a lei tocca.

SUSANNA *(fa una riverenza)*
No, no, tocca a lei.

(making a curtsy)
Go on, I'm your servant, magnificent lady.

SUSANNA *(making a curtsy)*
I should not presume too much, sharp-witted dame.

MARCELLINA *(making a curtsy)*
No, you go first.

SUSANNA *(making a curtsy)*
No, no, after you.

MARCELLINA *(fa una riverenza)*
No, prima a lei tocca.

SUSANNA *(fa una riverenza)*
No, no, tocca a lei.

MARCELLINA, SUSANNA
(fa fanno una riverenza)
Io so i dover miei, non fo inciviltà, ecc.

MARCELLINA *(fa una riverenza)*
La sposa novella!

SUSANNA *(fa una riverenza)*
La dama d'onore!

MARCELLINA *(fa una riverenza)*
De conte la bella!

SUSANNA
Di Spagna l'amore!

MARCELLINA
I meriti...

SUSANNA
L'abito!...

MARCELLINA
Il posto...

SUSANNA
L'età...

MARCELLINA
Per Bacco, precipito se ancor, se ancor resto
qua.

MARCELLINA *(making a curtsy)*
No, you go first.

SUSANNA *(making a curtsy)*
No, no, after you.

MARCELLINA, SUSANNA *(making a curtsy)*
I know my position, and do not breach
good manners, etc.

MARCELLINA *(making a curtsy)*
A bride-to-be!...

SUSANNA *(making a curtsy)*
A lady of honour...

MARCELLINA *(making a curtsy)*
The Count's favourite...

SUSANNA
All Spain's beloved...

MARCELLINA
Your merit...

SUSANNA
Your fine dress...

MARCELLINA
Your position...

SUSANNA
Your age...

MARCELLINA
By Bacchus, I might grow rash if I stay here
longer.

SUSANNA
Sibilla decrepita, da rider mi fa.

MARCELLINA (*fa una riverenza*)
Via, resti servita, ecc.

SUSANNA (*fa una riverenza*)
Non sono sì ardita, ecc.

MARCELLINA (*fa una riverenza*)
La sposa novella! ecc.

SUSANNA (*fa una riverenza*)
La dama d'onore! ecc.

(*Marcellina goes off in a rage*)

Recitativo

Va là, vecchia pedante, dottoressa arrogante, perchè hai letto due libri, e seccata Madama in gioventù...

(*Cherubino comes in*)

CHERUBINO
Susannetta, sei tu?

SUSANNA
Son io, cosa volete?

CHERUBINO
Ah, cor mio, che accidente!

SUSANNA
Cor vostro? Cosa avvenne?

SUSANNA
Decrepit old Sibyl, you make me laugh.

MARCELLINA (*making a curtsy*)
Go on, I'm your servant, etc.

SUSANNA (*making a curtsy*)
I should not presume so much, etc.

MARCELLINA (*making a curtsy*)
The bride-to-be, etc.

SUSANNA (*making a curtsy*)
A lady of honour, etc.

Go on, you old pedant, you ill-tempered schoolmistress, just because you've read two books and harassed Madame in her youth...

CHERUBINO
Little Susanna, is it you?

SUSANNA
It is I; what do you want?

CHERUBINO
Ah, my heart, what a misfortune!

SUSANNA
Your heart! What happened?

CHERUBINO

Il Conte ieri, perchè trovommi sol con Barbarina, il congedo mi diede, e se la Contessina, la mia bella comare, grazia non m'intercede, io vado via, io non ti vedo più, Susanna mia.

SUSANNA

Non vedete più me! Bravo! Ma dunque non più per la Contessa segretamente il vostro cor sospira?

CHERUBINO

Ah, che troppo rispetto ella m'inspira! Felice te, che puoi vederla quando vuoi, che la vesti il mattino, che la sera la spogli, che le metti gli spilloni, i merletti...Ah, se in tuo loco...Cos'hai lì? dimmi un poco...

SUSANNA

Ah, il vago nastro e la notturna cuffia di comare sì bella.

CHERUBINO

Deh dammelo, sorella, dammelo per pietà.

(he snatches the ribbon)

SUSANNA

Presto quel nastro.

CHERUBINO

Oh caro, oh bello, oh fortunato nastro! Io non te'l renderò che colla vita!

CHERUBINO

Yesterday, the Count, because he found me alone with Barbarina, gave me orders to go away: and if the dear Countess, my beloved protectress, doesn't grant her protection, I must go, and see you no more, my Susanna.

SUSANNA

See me no more! Bravo! So then it's not for the Countess now that your heart secretly yearns!

CHERUBINO

Ah, what great respect she inspires in me! Happy are you who can see her whenever you wish! You who dress her in the morning, you who undress her in the evening, pin up her hair, tie on her lace...Ah, to be in your place! What do you have there? Just tell me...

SUSANNA

Oh, just a pretty ribbon and the nightcap of your beautiful protectress.

CHERUBINO

Come, give it to me, my sister, give it to me for pity's sake.

SUSANNA

Quick, give it back.

CHERUBINO

O dearest, prettiest, most fortunate ribbon! I shall not give thee up, but with my life!

SUSANNA
Cos'è quest'insolenza?

CHERUBINO
Eh via, sta cheta! In ricompensa poi questa
mia canzonetta io ti vo' dare.

(he takes a song to the Countess outof his pocket)

SUSANNA *(cogliendo il foglio)*
E che ne debbo fare?

CHERUBINO
Leggila alla padrona; leggila tu medesma,
leggila a Barbarina, a Marcellina...leggila ad
ogni donna de' palazzo!

SUSANNA
Povero Cherubin, siete voi pazzo!

SUSANNA
What does this insolence mean?

CHERUBINO
Oh, please, don't tell! In payment I'll give
you this canzonetta of mine.

SUSANNA *(accepting it)*
And what would I do with it?

CHERUBINO
Read it to our patroness, read it to yourself,
read it to Barbarina, to Marcellina, read it
to every woman in the place!

SUSANNA
Poor Cherubino, are you mad!

disc no. 1/track 7

no. 6: Aria Here is Cherubino, the hormonally-driven youth who loves all
women (the role is one of the most famous of all "trouser roles," ie.: the part of
an adolescent boy sung by a female mezzo-soprano). The breathless quality of
this little aria again tells us as much about the character as the words—here is
an anxious, passionate, panting youth, ready to explore and explode.

CHERUBINO
Non so più cosa son, cosa faccio, or di
foco, ora sono di ghiaccio, ogni donna cangiar di colore, ogni donna mi fa palpitar.
Solo ai nomi d'amor, di diletto, mi sì turba,
mi s'altera il petto e a parlare mi sforza
d'amore un desio ch'io non posso spiegar.
Non so più cosa son, ecc. Parlo d'amor vegliando, parlo d'amor sognando, all'acqua,
all'ombre, ai monti, ai fiori, all'erbe, ai

CHERUBINO
I no longer know what I am, what I do;
now I'm all fire, now all ice; every woman
changes my temperature, every woman
makes my heart beat faster. The very men-
tion of love, of delight, disturbs me, changes
my heart, and speaking of love, forces on
me a desire I cannot restrain! I no longer
know what I am, etc. I speak of love while
I'm awake, I speak of love while I'm sleep-

fonti, all'eco, all'aria, ai venti, che il suon de' vani accenti portano via con sé. Parlo d'amor vegliando, ecc. E se non ho chi m'oda, parlo d'amor con me.

ing, to rivers, to shadows, to mountains, to flowers, to grass, to fountains, to echoes, to air, to winds, until they carry away the sound of my useless words. I speak of love while I'm awake, etc. And if no one is near to hear me I speak of love to myself.

(The Count's voice is heard outside. Cherubino dives behind the armchair)

Recitative

CHERUBINO
Ah! Son perduto! Che timor...Il Conte! Misera me!

CHERUBINO
Ah! I'm lost! How awful...It's the Count; how unlucky!

(the Count enters)

CONTE
Susanna, tu mi sembri agitata e confusa.

COUNT
Susanna, you seem nervous and confused.

SUSANNA
Signor...io chiedo scusa...ma, se mai qui sorpresa...per carità partite!

SUSANNA
Sir, I beg your pardon, but if someone... found you here; I beg you leave me.

(the Count sits on a chair; takes her hand)

CONTE
Un momento, e ti lascio. Odi.

COUNT
One moment, and I'll leave you. Listen.

SUSANNA
Non odo nulla.

SUSANNA
I won't hear anything.

CONTE
Due parole: tu sai che ambasciatore a Londra il re mi dichiarò: di condur meco Figaro destinai.

COUNT
Two words. You know that the king has appointed me ambassador to London; I have decided to take Figaro with me.

SUSANNA
Signor, se osassi...

CONTE
Parla, parla, mia cara! E con quel dritto,
ch'oggi prendi su me, finché tu vivi, chiedi,
imponi, prescrivi.

SUSANNA
Lasciatemi, signor, dritti non prendo, non
ne vo', non ne intendo. Oh me infelice!

CONTE
Ah, no, Susanna, io ti vo' far felice! Tu ben
sai quant'io t'amo; a te Basilio tutto già
disse, or senti se per pochi momenti meco
in giardin sull'imbrunir del giorno...ah per
questo favore io pagherei...

BASILIO *(dietro quinte)*
E uscito poco fa.

CONTE
Chi parla?

SUSANNA
Oh dei!

CONTE
Esci, ed alcun non entri.

SUSANNA
Ch'io vi lascio qui solo?

BASILIO *(sempre dietro quinte)*
Da Madama sarà, vado a cercarlo.

SUSANNA
Sir, if I dared...

COUNT
Speak, speak, my dear, and by that right
you assume today for as long as you live,
ask, request, demand.

SUSANNA
Leave me, signor; I am assuming no right
and do not intend to. Oh, unhappy me!

COUNT
Ah no, Susanna, I want to make you
happy! You know how much I love you.
Basilio has already told you everything.
Now listen. If for a few minutes you meet
me in the garden this evening...Ah, for this
favour I would pay...

BASILIO *(outside)*
He just left.

COUNT
Who is speaking?

SUSANNA
Ye gods!

COUNT
Go, and don't let anyone in...

SUSANNA
And leave you here alone?

BASILIO *(outside)*
He must be with Madame. I'll look for
him there.

CONTE (*additando la poltrona*)
Qui dietro mi porrò.

SUSANNA
Non vi celate.

CONTE
Taci, e cerca ch' parta.

SUSANNA
Ohimè! Che fate!

COUNT (*pointing to the chair*)
I can go behind this.

SUSANNA
Don't hide here.

COUNT
Hush, and try to get rid of him.

SUSANNA
Oh dear! What are you doing?

(the Count hides behind the chair. Cherubino, unobserved by him, scrambles into the seat and Susanna covers him with a dress as Basilio enters)

BASILIO
Susanna, il ciel vi salvi: avreste a caso veduto il Conte?

SUSANNA
E cosa deve far meco il Conte? Animo, uscite.

BASILIO
Aspettate, sentite, Figaro di lui cerca.

SUSANNA
(Oh cielo!) cerca chi dopo voi più l'odia.

CONTE
Vediam come me serve.

BASILIO
Io non ho mai nella moral sentito ch'uno ch'ama la moglie odii il marito, per dir che il Conte v'ama...

BASILIO
Susanna, Heaven bless you: have you by chance seen the Count?

SUSANNA
And what would the Count be doing here? Just go away!

BASILIO
Wait, and listen; Figaro is looking for him.

SUSANNA
(Heavens!) Then he's looking for the man who, after you, hates him most.

COUNT
We'll see how he serves me.

BASILIO
I've never heard any moral law that says that he who loves the wife must hate the husband. Which is to say that the Count loves you.

SUSANNA

Sortite, vil ministro dell'altrui sfrenatezza:
io non ho d'uopo della vostra morale, del
Conte, del suo amor...

BASILIO

Non c'è alcun male. Ha ciascuno i suoi
gusti; io mi credea che preferir doveste per
amante, come fan tutte quante, un signor
liberal, prudente e saggio, a un giovinastro,
a un paggio...

SUSANNA

A Cherubino!

BASILIO

A Cherbubino, a Cherubin d'amore, ch'oggi sul far del giorno passeggiava qui d'intorno per entrar.

SUSANNA

Uomo maligno, un'impostura è questa.

BASILIO

È un maligno con voi, chi ha gli occhi in
testa. E quella canzonetta, ditemi in confi-
denza, io sono amico, ed altrui nulla dico,
è per voi, per Madama?

SUSANNA

(Chi diavol gliel'ha detto?)

BASILIO

A proposito, figlia, istruitelo meglio, egli la
guarda a tavola sì spesso, e con tale immod-
estia che s'il Conte' s'accorge...e sul tal
punto, sapete, egli è una bestia.

SUSANNA

Get out, you pander to another's lascivious-
ness. I do not aspire to your system of
morality, nor to the Count's love.

BASILIO

There's no harm in it! Everyone to his own
taste; I should have thought that you
would prefer as a lover, as most women
would do, a generous gentleman, discreet
and wise, to a stripling, to a page...

SUSANNA

To Cherubino!

BASILIO

To Cherubino, love's cherubim, who today
at daybreak was seen on his way to this place.

SUSANNA

Wicked man! What a falsehood that is!

BASILIO

Is one evil just because one has eyes in his
head? And that canzonetta? Tell me, in
confidence: I am your friend and will tell
no one else: Is it for you? For Madame?

SUSANNA

(What devil told him about it?)

BASILIO

Apropos, my daughter, instruct him more
wisely; he stares at her so at the table, and
with such immodesty, that the Count is
beginning to notice: In this, you know, he
can be a terror.

SUSANNA
Scellerato! E perchè andate voi tai men-
zogne spargendo?

BASILIO
Io! Che ingiustizia! Quel che compro io
vendo, a quel che tutti dicono io non
aggiungo un pelo.

CONTE *(mostrandosi improvvisamente)*
Come! Che dicon tutti?

BASILIO
Oh bella!

SUSANNA
Oh cielo!

SUSANNA
Villain! And why do you come here to
spread such lies?

BASILIO
I! You do me wrong! What I sell, I also buy.
I have not added a hair to what everyone is
saying.

COUNT *(coming forward)*
How's that, what is everyone saying?

BASILIO
Oh, perfect!

SUSANNA
Oh, Heavens!

disc no. 1/track 8 *No. 7: Terzetto* The first of a number of great ensembles in the opera, we here discover how nasty the Count can be, how sniveling Basilio (the Music-Master) can be, and how well Susanna can react under pressure. Listening carefully to the text, one can also hear Basilio sing "Così fan tutte le belle" ("Women are all alike"): Is this the first notion Mozart and da Ponte had with regard to working together on an opera based on such a theme?

CONTE
Cosa sento! Tosto andate, e scacciate il
seduttor.

BASILIO
In mal punto son qui giunto; perdonate, o
mio signor.

SUSANNA
Che ruina, me meschina, son oppressa dal
terror!

COUNT
What do I hear! Go at once, and throw the
seducer out!

BASILIO
I came here at the wrong moment! Pardon
me, my Lord.

SUSANNA
I'm ruined, unhappy me! I'm crushed with
fright!

CONTE
Tosto andate, ecc.

BASILIO
In mal punto, ecc.

SUSANNA *(quasi svenuta)*
Che ruina, ecc.

CONTE, BASILIO *(sostenendola)*
Ah! Già svien la poverina! Come, oh Dio,
batte il cor, ecc.

BASILIO
Pian pianin, su questo seggio...

SUSANNA *(rinvenendo)*
Dove sono! Cosa veggio! Che insolenza,
andate fuor, ecc.

BASILIO
Siamo qui per aiutarvi, è sicuro il vostro
onor.

CONTE
Siamo qui per aiutarti, non turbarti, o mio
tesor.

BASILIO
Ah del paggio quel ch'ho detto, era solo un
mio sospetto.

SUSANNA
È un'insidia, una perfidia, non credete
all'impostor, ecc.

CONTE
Parta, parta il damerino, ecc.

COUNT
Go at once, etc.

BASILIO
At the wrong moment, etc.

SUSANNA *(she appears to faint)*
I'm ruined, etc.

COUNT, BASILIO *(supporting her)*
Ah, the poor dear is fainting! Oh God, how
her heart beats!

BASILIO
Softly, softly, on to this chair.

SUSANNA *(recovering and drawing away)*
Where am I? What is this? What insolence,
get out of here! etc.

BASILIO
We are here to help you, and your honour
is perfectly safe.

COUNT
We are here to help you; don't be alarmed,
my treasure.

BASILIO
Ah, what I said about the page was only a
suspicion of mine.

SUSANNA
It is a malicious scandal, don't believe the
impostor, etc.

COUNT
No, the young reprobate must go! etc.

SUSANNA, BASILIO
Poverino! ecc.

CONTE
Poverino! Poverino! Ma da me sorpreso ancor!

SUSANNA
Come?

BASILIO
Che?

SUSANNA
Che?

BASILIO
Come?

SUSANNA, BASILIO
Come? Che?

CONTE
Da tua cugina, l'uscio ier trovai rinchiuso;
picchio, m'apre Barbarina paurosa fuor del-
l'uso, io, dal muso insospettito, guardo,
cerco in ogni sito, ed alzando pian pianino
il tappeto al tavolino, vedo il paggio.

(he shows them what he means and lifting the dressing-gown on the chair discovers Cherubino)

Ah, Cosa veggio!

SUSANNA
Ah, crude stelle!

SUSANNA, BASILIO
Poor boy! etc.

COUNT
Poor boy? But I've caught him again!

SUSANNA
How's that?

BASILIO
What!

SUSANNA
What!

BASILIO
How's that?

SUSANNA, BASILIO
How's that? What?

COUNT
Yesterday I found your cousin's door was
locked; I knocked and Barbarina opened
much more sheepishly than usual. Suspicious
at her manner I went searching in every
corner, and raising up the table covering as
gently as you please, I found the page!

Ah, what's this I see?

SUSANNA
Ah, cruel fortune!

BASILIO
Ah, meglio ancora!

CONTE
Onestissima signora, or capisco come va!

SUSANNA
Accader non può di peggio; giusti Dei, che mai sarà!

BASILIO
Così fan tutte le belle non c'è alcuna novità! Ah, del paggio quel che ho detto era solo un mio sospetto..

CONTE
Basilio, in traccia tosto di Figaro volate; io vo' ch'ei veda...

SUSANNA
Ed io che senta; andate.

CONTE *(a Basilio)*
Restate, che baldanza! E Quale scusa se la colpa è evidente?

SUSANNA
Non ha d'uopo di scusa un'innocente.

CONTE
Ma costui quando venne?

SUSANNA
Egli era meco, quando voi qui giungeste. E mi chiedea d'impegnar la padrona a intercedergli grazia; il vostro arrivo in scompiglio lo pose, ed allor in quel loco sì nascose.

BASILIO
Ah, better yet!

COUNT
Most virtuous lady, now I understand your ways!

SUSANNA
It couldn't have turned out worse; ye just gods, what next!

BASILIO
All pretty women are the same, there's nothing new in this case! Ah, what I said about the page, was only a suspicion of mine.

COUNT
Basilio, take wing and track down Figaro this instant; I want him to see...

SUSANNA
And I want him to hear, go on.

COUNT *(to Basilio)*
Stay here: what nerve! What excuse is there if the facts are plain?

SUSANNA
Innocence needs no excuse.

COUNT
But when did this fellow come in?

SUSANNA
He was with me when you arrived, and was asking me to beg our patroness to intercede for him with you; your coming threw him into a panic, and he hid himself there.

CONTE
Ma s'io stesso m'assisi, quando in camera entrai!

CHERUBINO
Ed allora di dietro io mi celai.

CONTE
E quando io là mi posi?

CHERUBINO
Allor io pian mi volsi e qui m'ascosi.

CONTE
Oh ciel! Dunque ha sentito quello ch'io ti dicea!

CHERUBINO
Feci per non sentir quanto potea.

CONTE
Oh perfidia!

BASILIO
Frenatevi, vien gente.

CONTE
(a Cherubino)
E voi restate qui, picciol serpente.

No. 8: Chorus

(enter peasants, followed by Figaro with a white veil in his hand)

CORO
Giovani liete, fiori spargete davanti il nobile nostro signor. Il suo gran core vi serba intatto d'un più bel fiore l'almo candor.

COUNT
I myself sat there when I came into the room!

CHERUBINO
I was hiding behind it then.

COUNT
And when I went back there?

CHERUBINO
I slipped around quietly and got in here.

COUNT
Oh Heavens! Then he heard everything I said to you?

CHERUBINO
I tried as hard as I could not to hear.

COUNT
Wicked boy!

BASILIO
Control yourself, someone's coming.

COUNT *(to Cherubino)*
As for you, stay here, young serpent.

CHORUS
Carefree girls, scatter flowers before this noble master of ours. His great heart watches over you, the spotless flower of a noble soul.

CONTE
Cos'è questa commedia?

FIGARO *(piano, a Susanna)*
Eccoci in danza: secondami, cor mio.

SUSANNA
Non ci ho speranza.

FIGARO
Signor, non isdegnate questo del nostro
affetto meritato tributo: or che aboliste un
diritto sì ingrato a chi ben ama...

CONTE
Quel dritto or non v'è più, cosa sì brama?

FIGARO
Della vostra saggezza il primo frutto oggi
noi colgierem: le nostre nozze si son già sta-
bilite, or a voi tocca costei, che un vostro
dono illibata serbò, coprir di questa, sim-
bolo d'onestà, candida vesta.

CONTE *(tra sé)*
Diabolica astuzia! Ma fingere convien.
(forte)
Son grato, amici, ad un senso sì onesto! Ma
non merto per questo né tributi, né lodi, e
un dritto ingiusto ne miei feudi abolendo a
natura, al dover lor dritti io rendo.

COUNT
What is this farce?

FIGARO *(softly, to Susanna)*
Now is the time: stand behind me, dearest.

SUSANNA
It is useless.

FIGARO
Sir, do not spurn this expression of gratitude
you deserve so well: since you abolished a
lordly right so distasteful to all true lovers...

COUNT
That right no longer exists: what's the com-
motion?

FIGARO
We gather today the first fruit of your wis-
dom: our wedding is arranged, now it is
your duty to hand over your gift unspot-
ted, dressed in this symbol of honesty, pure
white raiment!

COUNT *(aside)*
Diabolical cleverness! But I must play the
game.
(aloud)
I welcome, friends, such good-hearted sen-
timents. But I deserve for this neither tribute
nor praise; by abolishing that unjust right
in my lands I only did my natural duty.

TUTTI
Evviva, evviva, evviva!

SUSANNA
Che virtù!

FIGARO
Che giustizia!

CONTE
A voi prometto compier la cerimonia.
Chiedo sol breve indugio: io voglio in faccia de' miei più fidi, e con più ricca pompa
rendervi appien felici.
(tra sé)
Marcellina, si trovi?
(forte)
Andate, amici.

No. 8a: Chorus

CORO
Giovani liete, fiori spargete, ecc.

(the peasants leave)

FIGARO
Evviva!

SUSANNA
Evviva!

BASILIO
Evviva!

FIGARO *(a Cherubino)*
E voi non applaudite?

ALL
Hurrah, hurrah, hurrah!

SUSANNA
What virtue!

FIGARO
What justice!

COUNT
I promise to fulfill the ceremony. I ask only
for your brief indulgence while I speak to
my most loyal subjects, and with the richest
of festivities I shall make you most happy.
(aside)
Marcellina, where are you?
(aloud)
Go forth, friends.

CHORUS
Carefree girls, etc.

FIGARO
Hurrah!

SUSANNA
Hurrah!

BASILIO
Hurrah!

FIGARO *(to Cherubino)*
And why aren't you cheering?

SUSANNA
È afflitto, poveretto, perché il padron lo scaccia dal castello.

FIGARO
Ah! In un giorno sì bello!

SUSANNA
In un giorno di nozze!

FIGARO *(al Conte)*
Quando ognuno v'ammira.

CHERUBINO
Perdono, mio signor.

CONTE
No! meritate.

SUSANNA
Egli è ancora fanciullo.

CONTE
Men di quel che tu credi.

CHERUBINO
È ver, mancai; ma dal mio labbro alfine...

CONTE
Ben, mio, io vi perdono; anzi farò di più, vacante è è un posto d'uffizial nel reggimento mio, io scelgo oi, voi, partite tosto, addio.

SUSANNA, FIGARO
Ah! Fin domani sol...

SUSANNA
He's saddened, poor boy, that hi master is chasing him out of the castle.

FIGARO
Ah, on such a beautiful day!

SUSANNA
On a wedding day!

FIGARO *(to the Count)*
When everyone is praising you!

CHERUBINO
Pardon, my lord!

COUNT
You don't deserve it.

SUSANNA
He's still a boy.

COUNT
Less so than you think.

CHERUBINO
True, I've been at fault; but now I swear...

COUNT
Very well; I pardon you. I will do even more: there is vacant an officer's post in my regiment; you may have it; go immediately; farewell.

SUSANNA, FIGARO
Ah! Tomorrow morning!

CONTE
No, parta tosto.

COUNT
No, he goes now.

CHERUBINO
A ubbidirvi, signor, son già disposto.

CHERUBINO
Sir, I am ready to obey you.

CONTE
Via, per l'ultima volta la Susanna abbracciate.
(tra sé)
Inaspettato è il colpo.

COUNT
Go then, for the last time embrace your Susanna.
(aside)
The blow was unexpected.

(the Count and Basilio leave)

FIGARO
Ehi, capitano, a me pure la mano. Io vo' parlarti pria che tu parta. Addio, picciolo Cherubino! Come cangia in un punto il tuo destino!

FIGARO
Well, captain, give me your hand. I want to speak to you before you depart. Farewell, little Cherubino; how your destiny has changed in a moment!

disc no. 1/track 9 *no. 9: Aria* This is the opera's first big hit, one that was such a resounding smash that Mozart used it again in Don Giovanni in an irresistible, self-referential way. In it, Figaro bids formal farewell to Cherubino as the youth is about to embark on an uninvited, unwanted military career—little can be said about this tune other than it finds the opera (and Mozart) at its most mischievous and captivating, all in a jaunty march rhythm.

Non più andrai, farfallone amoroso, notte e giorno d'intorno girando, delle belle turbando il riposo, Narcisetto, Adoncino d'amor, ecc. Non più avrai questi bei pennacchini, quel cappello leggiero e galante, quella chioma, quell'aria brillante, quel vermiglio donnesco color. Non più andrai, ecc. Tra guerrieri poffar Bacco! Gran mustacchi, stretto sacco, schioppo in spalla,

No more will you, amorous butterfly, flit around the castle night and day, upsetting all the pretty girls, love's little Narcissus and Adonis, etc. No more will you have those fine plumes, that soft and stylish hat, those fine locks, that striking air, those rosy, girl-like cheeks. No more will you, etc. Among warriors swearing by Bacchus! great mustacchios, holding your pack, a

sciabola al fianco, col'o dritto, muso fran-
co, o un gran casco, o un gran turbante,
molto onor, poco contante, ed invece del
fandango, una marcia per il fango, per
montagne, per valloni, colle nevi, e i
solleoni, al concerto di tromboni, di bom-
barde, di cannoni, che le palle in tutti i
tuoni all'orecchio fan fischiar. Cherubino
alla vittoria, alla gloria militar!

gun on your shoulder, a sabre hanging at
your right, musket ready, or some great
helmet or a turban, winning honours, but
little money, and in place of the fandango a
march through the mud. Over mountains,
over valleys, through the snow and burning
sun. To the music of trumpets, of shells
and cannons, with balls sounding thunder,
making your ears ring. Cherubino, on to
victory, on to victory in war!

(they leave, marching like soldiers)

Act 2

The Countess's boudoir

disc no. 1/track 10 *No. 10: Cavatina* The only thing missing from the opera so far is its most sympathetic character—what a terrific move on Mozart's part (letters attribute the idea to composer, not librettist)! Here the Countess sings an inward, calm plea—to love, disembodied—to return her husband's love to her, or to allow her to die.

(To the right is a door, to the left of a closet. A door at the back leads to the servants' rooms; on one side, a window. The Countess is alone)

CONTESSA
Porgi, amor, qualche ristoro, al mio duolo,
a' miei sospir! O mi rendi il mio tesoro, o
mi lascia almen morir! Porgi amor, ecc.

COUNTESS
Grant, love, that relief to my sorrow, to my
sighing. Give me back my treasure, or at
least let me die. Grant, love, etc.

(Susanna comes in)

Recitative

Vieni, cara Susanna, finiscimi l'istoria.

Come, dear Susanna, finish the story.

SUSANNA
È già finita.

SUSANNA
It's already finished.

CONTESSA
Dunque volle sedurti?

COUNTESS
Then he tried to seduce you?

SUSANNA
Oh, il signor Conte non fa tai complimenti
colle donne mie pari; egli venne a contratto
di danari.

CONTESSA
Ah! il crudel più non m'ama!

SUSANNA
E come poi è geloso di voi?

CONTESSA
Come lo sono i moderni mariti! Per sister-
ma infedeli, per genio capricciosi e per
orgoglio poi tutti gelosi. Ma se Figaro
t'ama ei sol potria...

FIGARO (entrando)
La, la, la, la, la, la...

SUSANNA
Eccolo; vieni, amico, Madama
impaziente...

FIGARO
A voi non tocca stare in pena per questo.
Alfin di che si tratta? Al signor Conte piace
la sposa mia; indi segretamente ricuperar
vorria il diritto feudale; possibile è la cosa e
naturale.

CONTESSA
Possibil?

SUSANNA
Natural?

SUSANNA
Oh, his lordship pays no such compliments
to women of my rank; he only thinks of it
as a business matter.

COUNTESS
Ah! The cruel man loves me no more!

SUSANNA
Then why is he so jealous of you?

COUNTESS
That's how all modern husbands are! Sys-
tematically unfaithful, brilliantly capricious, and out of vanity all jealousy. But if
Figaro loves you only he can...

FIGARO (singing as he enters)
La, la, la, la, la, la...

SUSANNA
Here he is; come, my friend, madame is
getting impatient...

FIGARO
Madame, you should not concern yourself
in this matter. In short, what does it come
to? The Count is pleased with my bride,
and through her he means to recoup his
feudal right; it's all possible, and natural.

COUNTESS
Possible?

SUSANNA
Natural?

FIGARO

Naturalissima, e se Susanna vuol, possibilissima.

SUSANNA

Finiscila una volta.

FIGARO

Ho già finito. Quindi, prese il partito di sceglier me corriero, e la Susanna consigliera segreta d'ambasciata; e perch'ella ostinata ognor rifiuta il diploma d'onor che le destina, minaccia di protegger Marcellina; questo è tutto l'affare.

SUSANNA

Ed hai coraggio di trattar scherzando un negozio sì serio?

FIGARO

Non vi basta che scherzando io ci pensi? Ecco il progetto: per Basilio un biglietto io gli fo' capitar, che l'avvertisca di certo appuntamento, che per l'ora del ballo a un amante voi deste...

CONTESSA

Oh ciel! Che sento! Ad un uom sì geloso...

FIGARO

Ancora meglio, così potrem più presto imbarazzarlo, confonderlo, imbrogliarlo, rovesciargli i progetti, empierlo di sospetti, e porgli in testa che la moderna festa ch'ei di fare a me tenta, altri a lui faccia. Onde qua perda il tempo, ivi la traccia, così quasi

FIGARO

Most natural, and if Susanna agrees, most possible.

SUSANNA

Finish your story.

FIGARO

I've already finished. Therefore he has decided to choose me as his courier, and Susanna secret counsellor of the embassy; and since she has stubbornly refused the high credentials destined for her, he threatens to favour Marcellina; that's the whole situation.

SUSANNA

And you have the nerve to joke about such a serious matter?

FIGARO

Isn't it enough that I think while I joke? Here's my plan: With Basilio's help I'll see that he finds a letter informing him of a certain assignation while the ball is going on between you and your lover.

COUNTESS

Heavens! What are you saying? With such a jealous man!

FIGARO

All the better, that way we can embarrass him faster, confound him, entangle him, upset his schemes, banish his suspicions, and make him know that another can play this modern game he's trying to play. And so we'll gain time, as I've planned it, and ex

ex abrupto e senza ch'abbia fatto per fras-
tornarci alcun disegno vien l'ora delle
nozze, e in faccia a lei non fia ch'osi d'op-
porsi ai voti miei.

SUSANNA
È ver, ma in di lui vece s'opporrà Marcellina.

FIGARO
Aspetta! Al Conte farai subito dir che verso
sera attendati in giardino. Il picciol Cherubino, per mio consiglio non ancor partito,
da femmina vestito, faremo che in sua vece
ivi sen vada; questa è l'unica strada, onde
Monsù, sorpresioda Madama, sia costretto
a far poi quel che si brama.

CONTESSA
Che ti par?

SUSANNA
Non c'è mal.

CONTESSA
Nel nostro caso...

SUSANNA
Quand'egli è persuaso...

CONTESSA
E dove è il tempo?

FIGARO
Ito è il Conte alla caccia, e per qualch'ora non
sarà di ritorno. Io vado, e tosto Cherubino

abrupto, you might say, and if nothing happens to disturb our plans, the hour will come
for the wedding, and with Madame on our
side, he won't dare to prevent our vows.

SUSANNA
True, but in his place Marcellina will rear
her head.

FIGARO
Wait! Immediately I'll let the Count know
that toward evening you will be waiting for
him in the garden. Little Cherubino, upon
my advice, hasn't left yet, and in female
attire we'll have him here in your place.
This is the only way whereby Monsieur,
discovered by Madame, can be forced to
practise what he preaches.

COUNTESS
What do you think?

SUSANNA
Not bad.

COUNTESS
In our position...

SUSANNA
If he can be persuaded...

COUNTESS
Is there time?

FIGARO
The Count has gone hunting, and won't
return for about an hour. I'll go, and right

vi mando; lascio a voi la cura di vestirlo.

CONTESSA
E poi?

FIGARO
E poi? Se vuol ballare, signor contino, il chitarrino le suonerò, sì, ecc.

(he leaves)

CONTESSA
Quanto duolmi, Susanna, che questo giovinotto abbia del Conte le stravaganze udite! Ah! Tu non sai! Ma per qual causa mai da me stessa ei non venne? Dov'è la canzonetta?

SUSANNA
Eccola, appunto facciam che ce la canti. Zitto, vien gente; è desso; avanti, avant, signor uffiziale.

(Cherubino enters)

CHERUBINO
Ah, non chiamarmi con nome sì fatale! Ei mi rammenta che abbandonar degg'io comare tanto buona.

SUSANNA
E tanto bella!

CHERUBINO
Ah, sì certo.

away send Cherubino to you. I leave to you the job of dressing him.

COUNTESS
And then?

FIGARO
And then? If you would dance, my pretty Count, I'll play the tune on my little guitar, etc.

COUNTESS
How it pains me, Susanna, that this youth heard the foolish words of the Count! Ah! You can't imagine! But why in the world didn't he come to see me himself? Where is the canzonetta?

SUSANNA
Here it is; in fact let's make him sing it for you. Quickly, someone's coming. It's he; forward. Sir Officer!

CHERUBINO
Ah, don't call me by that awful name! It reminds me that I must abandon such a generous protectress.

SUSANNA
And beautiful?

CHERUBINO
Ah, yes, certainly.

SUSANNA
Ah, sì certo; ipocritone! Via. presto, la canzone che stamane a me deste, a Madama cantate.

SUSANNA
Ah, yes, certainly. Hypocrite! Now quickly, the poem that you read for me this morning, sing it for Madame.

CONTESSA
Chi n'è l'autor?

COUNTESS
Who is the author?

SUSANNA
Guardate, egli ha due brace di rossor sulla faccia.

SUSANNA
Look, there are two streaks of red on his cheeks.

CONTESSA
Prendi la mia chitarra, e l'accompagna.

COUNTESS
Take my guitar and accompany him.

CHERUBINO
Lo sono sì tremante; ma se Madama vuole...

CHERUBINO
I am so nervous; but if Madame desires...

SUSANNA
Lo vuole, sì, lo vuol. Manco parole.

SUSANNA
She does desire it. Enough with words.

disc no. 1/track 12 *No. 11. Canzona* Art within art emerges here: Cherubino meekly sings a song he's composed about love (what else?) and we (and the Countess and Susanna) are bowled over by its directness, its simplicity. Who wouldn't feel for this guy?

CHERUBINO
Voi, che sapete che cosa è amor, donne vedete, s'io l'ho nel cor. Quello ch'io provo, vi ridirò, e per me nuovo, capir nol so. Sento un affetto pien di desir, ch'ora è diletto, ch'ora è martir. Gelo, e poi sento l'alma avvampar, e in un momento torno a gelar. Ricerco un bene fuori di me, non so chi 'l tiene, non so cos'è. Sospiro e gemo senza voler, palpito e tremo senza saper;

CHERUBINO
You who know what love is, ladies, see whether it's in my heart. What I experience I'll describe for you; it's new to me, I don't understand it. I feel an emotion full of desire, that is now pleasure, and now suffering. I freeze, then I feel my soul burning up, and in a moment I'm freezing again. I seek a blessing outside myself, from whom I know not or what it is. I sigh and moan

non trovo pace notte, né dì, ma pur mi
piace languir così. Voi, che sapete, ecc.

Recitative

CONTESSA
Bravo! Che bella voce! Io non sapea che
cantaste sì bene.

SUSANNA
Oh in verità, egli fa tutto ben quello ch'ei fa.
Presto, a noi, bel soldato: Figaro v'informò...

CHERUBINO
Tutto mi disse.

SUSANNA
Laciatemi veder: andrà benissimi: siam
d'uguale statura...giù quel manto.

CONTESSA
Che fai?

SUSANNA
Niente paura.

CONTESSA
E se qualcuno entrasse?

SUSANNA
Entri, che mal facciamo? La porta chiuderò. Ma come poi acconciargli i capelli?

(she closes the door)

without meaning to, palpitate and tremble
without knowing it. I find no peace night
or day, and yet I enjoy languishing so. You
who know what love is, etc.

COUNTESS
Bravo! What a fine voice! I didn't know you
sang so well!

SUSANNA
Oh, truly, he does everything well. Quickly,
come here, handsome soldier. Figaro told you?

CHERUBINO
He told me all.

SUSANNA
Let me see; it will work very well, we're the
same height. Off with your coat.

COUNTESS
What are you doing?

SUSANNA
Don't be afraid.

COUNTESS
And if someone came in?

SUSANNA
Let him come, what are we doing wrong? I'll
shut the door. But how can we do his hair?

CONTESSA
Una mia cuffia prendi nel gabinetto.
Presto!

COUNTESS
Get one of my caps out of the closet.
Quickly!

(Susanna goes into the dressing room)

Che carta è quella?

What paper is that?

CHERUBINO
La patente.

CHERUBINO
My commission.

CONTESSA
Che sollecita gente!

COUNTESS
What solicitous people!

CHERUBINO
L'ebbi or or da Basilio.

CHERUBINO
I just got it from Basilio.

CONTESSA
Dalla freetta obliato hanno il sigillo.

COUNTESS
In their hurry they forgot the seal.

SUSANNA *(tornando)*
Il sigillo di che?

SUSANNA *(returning)*
The seal for what?

CONTESSA
Della patente.

COUNTESS
For the commission.

SUSANNA
Cospetto! Che premura! Ecco la cuffia.

SUSANNA
Good lord, What haste! Here is the cap.

CONTESSA
Spicciati; va bene; miserabili noi, se il
Conte viene.

COUNTESS
Hurry, we still have time. Unlucky us if the
Count comes.

No. 12: Aria

SUSANNA

Venite, inginocchiatevi, restate fermo li!
Pian, piano, or via giratevi, bravo, va ben
così, la faccia ora volgetemi, olà! Quegli
occhi a me, drittissimo, guardatemi,
Madama qui non è. Più alto quel colletto,
quel ciglio un po' più basso, le mani sotto il
petto, vedremo poscia il passo quando
sarete in piè. Mirate il bricconcello, mirate
quanto è bello! Che furba guardatura, che
vezzo, che figura! Se l'amano le femmine,
han certo il lor perché.

SUSANNA

Come here, get down on your knees, and
stay still there! Gently, now turn around
again. Bravo, that's just fine. Now turn
your face around, ha! Don't make such eyes
at me; keep looking straight on ahead,
Madame is not there. Pull this collar a bit
higher, keep your eyes down lower, your
hands across your chest, we'll see how you
walk when you're on your feet. Look at the
little colt, look how handsome he is! What
a crafty expression, what an outfit, what a
figure! If women fall in love with him, they
have their reasons why.

Recitative

CONTESSA

Quante buffonerie!

COUNTESS

What foolishness!

SUSANNA

Ma se ne sono io medesma gelosa! Ehi! ser-
pentello, volete tralasciar d'esser sì bello?

SUSANNA

I'm even jealous myself! Hey! You little serpent, will you stop being so handsome?

CONTESSA

Finiam le ragazzate; or quelle maniche oltre
il gomito gli alza, onde più agiatamente
l'abito gli si adatti.

COUNTESS

Let's finish these pranks. Now lift his
sleeves up above his elbows so that the
dress can be fitted more comfortably.

SUSANNA *(eseguendo)*
Ecco!

SUSANNA *(raising the sleeve)*
There!

CONTESSA

Più indietro, così; che nastro è quello?

COUNTESS

Further back, there; what is this ribbon?

SUSANNA

È quel ch'esso involommi.

SUSANNA

It's the one he stole from me.

CONTESSA (*snodando il nastro*)
E questo sangue?

CHERUBINO
Quel sangue...io non so come, poco pria
sdrucciolando...in un sasso la pelle io mi
sgraffiai...e la piaga col nastro io mi fasciai.

SUSANNA
Mostrate: non è mal; cospetto! Ha il braccio più candido del mio! Qualche ragazza...

CONTESSA
E segui a far la pazza? Va nel mio gabinetto,
e prendi un poco d'inglese taffetà, ch'è
sullo scrigno.

(Susanna goes into the dressing room)

In quanto al nastro...inver...per il colore mi
spiacea di privarmene.

SUSANNA (*rientrando*)
Tenete, e da legargli il braccio?

CONTESSA
Un altro nastro prendi insiem col mio
vestito.

(Susanna goes off through the door at the back with the page's cloak)

CHERUBINO
Ah! Più presto m'avria quello guarito!

CONTESSA
Perchè? Questo è migliore.

COUNTESS (*taking the ribbon*)
And this blood?

CHERUBINO
That blood...I don't know how but I slipped
a while ago...on a rock...I scratched the skin...
and I bound the wound with the ribbon.

SUSANNA
Let's see it: it's not bad. Look here! His arm
is whiter than mine; like a girl's...

COUNTESS
Are you still playing games? Go into my
closet, and bring out some sticking plaster
– it's on the jewel box.

As for the ribbon...really...because of the
colour, I'd be sorry to lose it.

SUSANNA (*reappearing*)
Wait, how will we bind up his arm?

COUNTESS
Bring another ribbon with the dress.

CHERUBINO
Ah! That one would have healed me sooner!

COUNTESS
Why? This one is finer.

CHERUBINO
Allor che un nastro...legò la chioma...ovver toccò la pelle...d'oggetto...

CONTESSA
Forestiero, è buon per le ferite, non è vero? Guardate qualità ch'io non sapea!

CHERUBINO
Madama scherza, ed io frattanto parto.

CONTESSA
Poverin! Che sventura!

CHERUBINO
Oh me infelice!

CONTESSA
Or piange...

CHERUBINO
Oh ciel! Perché morir non lice! forse vicino all'ultimo momento...questa bocca oseria...

CONTESSA
Siate saggio, cos'è questa follia?

(hearing a knock at the door)

Chi picchia alla mia porta?

CONTE *(fuori)*
Perché chiusa?

CONTESSA
Il mio sposo! Oh Dei! Son morta. Voi qui senza mantello! In questo stato...un ricevu-

CHERUBINO
Because the ribbon...that has tied the hair...or touched the skin...of one whom...

COUNTESS
...someone else, it's good for wounds, is it? It possesses qualities I never suspected!

CHERUBINO
Madame is joking, and I must leave.

COUNTESS
Poor boy! How unhappy!

CHERUBINO
Oh miserable me!

COUNTESS
Now he's weeping...

CHERUBINO
Heavens! Why can't I die! Perhaps at my last moment...this mouth might dare...

COUNTESS
Are you mad? What is this nonsense?

Who is beating at my door?

COUNT *(outside)*
Why is it shut?

COUNTESS
My husband! Ye gods! I'm finished! And you without a coat! In here dressed like

to foglio, la sua gran gelosia...

CONTE
Cosa indugiate?

CONTESSA
Son sola...ah sì...son sola...

CONTE
E a chi parlate?

CONTESSA
A voi...certo, a voi stesso.

CHERUBINO
Dopo quel ch'è successo...il suo
furore...non trovo altro consiglio...

(he runs and hides in the dressing room)

CONTESSA
Ah! Mi difenda il cielo in tal periglio!

(the Countess takes the key of the dressing room then goes to admit the Count)

CONTE
Che novità! Non fu mai vostra usanza di
rinchiudervi in stanza.

CONTESSA
È ver; ma...io stava qui mettendo...

CONTE
Via, mettendo...

CONTESSA
Certe robe; era meco la Susanna, che in sua
camera è andata.

that...Figaro's letter...his tremendous jealousy!

COUNT
What's taking so long?

COUNTESS
I am alone...yes...I am alone...

COUNT
Whom are you talking to?

COUNTESS
To you...of course, to you.

CHERUBINO
After what has happened, and his anger, I
have no other alternative!

COUNTESS
Ah, Heaven defend me in such danger!

COUNT
This is new! You never used to lock yourself in your room!

COUNTESS
True; but I...I was here putting away...

COUNT
Go on, putting away...

COUNTESS
some robes; Susanna was with me, but she
has gone into her own room.

CONTE
Ad ogni modo voi non siete tranquilla.
Guardate questo foglio.

CONTESSA *(tra sé)*
Numi! È il foglio che Figaro gli scrisse.

(Cherubino knocks against a chair in the dressing room)

CONTE
Cos'è codesto strepito? In gabinetto
qualche cosa è caduta.

CONTESSA
Io non intesi niente.

CONTE
Convien che abbiate i gran pensieri in
mente.

CONTESSA
Di che?

CONTE
Là v'è qualcuno.

CONTESSA
Chi volete che sia?

CONTE
Lo chiedo a voi; io vengo in questo punto.

CONTESSA
Ah sì...Susanna...appunto...

CONTE
Che passò, mi diceste, alla sua stanza.

COUNT
At any rate, you are not very calm. Look at
this letter.

COUNTESS *(aside)*
Ye gods! It's the letter Figaro wrote him!

COUNT
What's that uproar? Something fell down
in the closet.

COUNTESS
I heard nothing.

COUNT
You must have important thoughts in your
head.

COUNTESS
About what?

COUNT
Someone's in there.

COUNTESS
Who could it be!

COUNT
You tell me. I have just arrived.

COUNTESS
Ah yes, Susanna, certainly.

COUNT
Didn't you say she went into her own room?

CONTESSA
Alla sua stanza, o qui, non vidi bene.

CONTE
Susanna, e donde viene che siete sì turbata?

CONTESSA
Per la mia cameriera?

CONTE
Io non so nulla; ma turbata senz'altro.

CONTESSA
Ah questa serva più che non tuba me,
turba voi stesso.

CONTE
È vero, è vero! E lo vedrete adesso.

(Susanna enters through the door at the back and stops as she sees the Count who has not seen her)

No. 13: Terzetto

(knocking on the door of the closet)

Susanna, or via sortite, sortite, così vo?

CONTESSA
Fermatevi, sentite, sortire ella non può,

SUSANNA
Cos'è codesta lite? il paggio dove andò?

CONTE
E chi vietarlo or osa? Chi?

COUNTESS
To her room or in there, I didn't notice.

COUNT
Susanna! And how is it that you are so upset?

COUNTESS
On account of my maid?

COUNT
I don't know, but certainly upset.

COUNTESS
Ah, this girl has you more upset than me.

COUNT
True, true, and now you'll witness it.

Susanna, now, come out. Come out, I order you.

COUNTESS
Wait, and listen; she cannot come out.

SUSANNA
What has happened? Where has the page gone?

COUNT
And who dares to forbid it? Who?

CONTESSA
Lo vieta, lo vieta l'onestà. Un abito da
sposa provando ella si sta.

CONTE
Chiarissima è la cosa, l'amante qui sarà, ecc.

CONTESSA
Bruttissima è la cosa, chi sa, cosa sarà, ecc.

SUSANNA
Capisco qualche cosa, veggiamo come va, ecc.

CONTE
Susanna,

CONTESSA
Fermatevi!

CONTE
or via sortite!

CONTESSA
Sentite!

CONTE
Sortite!

CONTESSA
Fermatevi!

CONTE
Io così vo'!

CONTESSA
Sortire ella non può.

COUNTESS
Modesty forbids it. She's in there trying on
her new gown for the wedding.

COUNT
The matter's quite clear: her lover is in there.

COUNTESS
A brutal situation: who knows what will
come of it?

SUSANNA
I think I understand. Let's see what happens.

COUNT
Susanna,

COUNTESS
Wait!

COUNT
come out!

COUNTESS
Listen!

COUNT
Come out!

COUNTESS
Wait!

COUNT
I order you!

COUNTESS
She cannot come out.

CONTE
Dunque parlate almeno, Susanna, se qui siete?

CONTESSA
Nemmen, nemmen, nemmeno, io v'ordino, tacete.

CONTE
Consorte mia, giudizio, un scandalo, un disordine, schiviam per carità!

SUSANNA
Oh ciel! Un precipizio, un scandalo, un disordine, qui certo nascerà!

CONTESSA
Consorte mio, giudizio, un scandalo, un disordine, schiviam per carità!

Recitative

CONTE
Dunque voi non aprite?

CONTESSA
E perché deggio le mie camere aprir?

CONTE
Ebben lasciate, l'aprirem senza chiavi. Ehi, gente.

CONTESSA
Come? Porreste a repentaglio d'una dama l'onore?

COUNT
Well then, speak at least, Susanna, if you're in there.

COUNTESS
No, no, no, no, no, no, I order you to be quiet.

COUNT
My wife, be reasonable, a scandal, an uproar, can be avoided, I beg you!

SUSANNA
Heavens! A disaster, a scandal, an uproar, will certainly result!

COUNTESS
My Lord, be reasonable, a scandal, an uproar, can be avoided, I beg you!

COUNT
Then you won't open?

COUNTESS
And why should I open my own chambers?

COUNT
Very well, then, we'll open it without a key. Ho, servants!

COUNTESS
How's that? Would you play games with a lady's honour?

CONTE
È vero, io sbaglio, posso senza rumore, senza scandalo alcun di nostra gente, andar io stesso a prender l'occorrente. Attendete pur qui - ma perché in tutto sia il mio dubbio distrutto anco le porte io prima chiuderò.

(he locks Susanna's door)

CONTESSA
Che imprudenza.

CONTE
Vio la condiscendenza di venir meco avrete. Madama, eccovi il braccio, andiamo!

CONTESSA
Andiamo!

CONTE
Susanna starà qui finché torniamo.

(they leave. Susanna rushes out of the alcove where she had been hiding, and runs to the closet door)

No 14: Duettino

SUSANNA
Aprite, presto, aprite, aprite, è la Susanna; sortite, via sortite andate via di qua.

CHERUBINO *(escendo tutto confuso)*
Ohimè, che scena orribile! Che gran fatalità!

COUNT
You're right. I lost my head. I can, without noise, without a scandal among our people, go after the necessary equipment. Wait here...but no: to completely satisfy my doubts I'll even shut the door first.

COUNTESS
What foolhardiness.

COUNT
Please condescend to accompany me. Madame, here is my arm. Let us go.

COUNTESS
Let us go.

COUNT
Susanna will be here when we return.

SUSANNA
Open, quickly, open; open, it's Susanna. Come out, now, come out, come on out of there.

CHERUBINO *(entering, confused and out of breath)*
Oh dear, what a terrible scene! What a disaster!

SUSANNA
Di qua...di là...

CHERUBINO
Che gran fatalità!

SUSANNA, CHERUBINO
Le porte son serrate, che mai sarà?

CHERUBINO
Qui perdersi non giova.

SUSANNA
V'uccide se vi trova.

CHERUBINO *(appressandosi alla finestra)*
Veggiamo un po' qui fuori,

(getting ready to jump)

dà proprio nel giardino.

SUSANNA *(trattenendolo)*
Fermate, Cherubino, fermate, per pietà!

CHERUBINO
Qui perdersi non giova,

SUSANNA
Fermate, Cherubino,

CHERUBINO
m'uccide se mi trova,

SUSANNA
Tropp'alto per un salto. Fermate per pietà!

SUSANNA
This way, that way...

CHERUBINO
What a disaster!

SUSANNA, CHERUBINO
The doors are locked, What will happen next?

CHERUBINO
No use to stay here.

SUSANNA
He'll kill you if he finds you.

CHERUBINO *(looking out of the window)*
Look down here a moment,

it opens on the garden.

SUSANNA *(restraining him)*
Wait, Cherubino, wait, for pity's sake!

CHERUBINO
No use to stay here,

SUSANNA
Wait, Cherubino!

CHERUBINO
he'll kill me if he finds me,

SUSANNA
It's too high to jump. Wait, for pity's sake!

CHERUBINO
Lasciami, lasciami! Pria di nuocerle, nel
foco volerei! Abbraccio te per lei! Addio!
Così si fa!

(he jumps out of the window)

SUSANNA
Ei va a perire, oh dei! Fermate per pietà!

(she runs to the window)

Recitative
Oh guarda il demonietto come fugge! È già
un miglio lontano; ma non perdiamci
invano: entriam nel gabinetto; venga poi lo
smargiasso, io qui l'aspetto.

CHERUBINO
Leave me, leave me! To save her I would
leap into flames! I embrace you for her!
Farewell! So be it.

SUSANNA
He'll kill himself, ye gods! Wait, for pity's sake!

Oh, look at the little devil! How he flies!
He's a mile away already! But let's not lose
everything. I'll go into the closet. Then
when the bully comes, I'll be waiting.

(she goes into the dressing room. The Count enters with the Countess)

CONTE
Tutto è come il lasciai: volete dunque aprir
voi stessa, o deggio...

CONTESSA
Ahimè! Fermate, e ascoltatemi un poco: mi
credete capace di mancar al dover?

CONTE
Come vi piace, entro quel gabinetto chi v'è
chiuso vedrò.

CONTESSA
Sì, lo vedrete, ma uditemi tranquillo.

CONTE
Non è dunque Susanna?

COUNT
Everything is as we left it; now do you wish
to open it yourself, or must I...

COUNTESS
Ah, wait, and listen to me a moment. Do
you think me capable of failing in my duty.

COUNT
Whatever you say, I'm going into that closet to see who is shut up inside.

COUNTESS
Yes, you'll see. But listen to me calmly.

COUNT
Then it's not Susanna?

CONTESSA
No, ma invece è un oggetto che ragion di
sospetto non vi deve lasciar: per questa sera...
una burla innocente...di farsi disponeva...
ed io vi giuro chel'onor...l'onestà...

COUNTESS
No, instead it's something that because of
your suspicions I can't let you see: for this
evening...we are planning an innocent prank...
and I swear that my honour...my purity...

CONTE
Chi è dunque? dite...L'ucciderò.

COUNT
Who is it then? Say...I'll kill him.

CONTESSA
Sentite...ah non ho cor!

COUNTESS
Listen...ah, I haven't the heart!

CONTE
Parlate!

COUNT
Speak!

CONTESSA
È un fanciullo...

COUNTESS
It is a boy.

CONTE
Un fanciul?

COUNT
A boy?

CONTESSA
Sì...Cherubino...

COUNTESS
Yes...Cherubino...

CONTE
E mi farà il destino ritrovar questo paggio
in ogni loco! Come? Non è partito?
Scellerati! Ecco i dubbi spiegati, ecco l'imbroglio, ecco il raggiro onde m'avverte il
foglio.

COUNT
Then it is my destiny to find that page
everywhere I go! How's that? He hasn't left?
Villains! These are my justified suspicions,
here's the mess, the plot of which the letter
warned me.

disk no. 1/
tracks 20-24 *no. 15: Finale* Here begins 20-or-so minutes of the greatest—and most
entertaining—music ever penned. Mozart invented the form of this finale, in
which a duet turns into a trio, which, in turm, becomes a quartet, and so on,
with the rhythm changing even more often than the number of characters and
the tension, albeit comic tension, mounting by the minute. By the time it's over
every character has been, at one time or another, tickled by the turns of events.

Susanna has had to navigate some very tricky waters, (at track 23) the drunken gardener, Antonio, enters and almost destroys all of Susanna's and the Countess's plotting, Figaro, after almost giving away the ruse, begins to take an active part in it and saves it, and (at track 24) as if the confusion weren't rich enough, Marcellina, Basilio and Bartolo enter and publicly announce that in order to pay off an old debt, Figaro has to marry Marcellina. The act ends with the trio of Susanna, Figaro and the Countess absolutely stupefied and the quartet of Marcellina, the Count, Basilio and Bartolo gloating—all at the same time. It doesn't get much better than this.

(going impetuously to the door of the dressing room)

Esci ormai, garzon malnato, sciagurato, non tardar.

If you're coming out, low-born brat, you wretch, don't be slow about it.

CONTESSA
Ah! signore, quel furore, per lui fammi il cor tremar.

COUNTESS
Ah sir, your anger makes my heart tremble for him.

CONTE
E d'opporvi ancor osate?

COUNT
And yet you dare to oppose me?

CONTESSA
No, sentite.

COUNTESS
No, listen.

CONTE
Via parlate!

COUNT
Go on, speak!

CONTESSA
Giuro al ciel, ch'ogni sospetto...e lo stato in che il trovate, sciolto il collo, nudo il petto...

COUNTESS
I swear by Heaven, that every suspicion, and the state in which you'll find him, his collar loosened, his chest bare...

CONTE
Sciolto il collo! Nudo il petto! Seguitate!

COUNT
Collar loosened, his chest bare...go on!

CONTESSA
Per vestir femminee spoglie...

CONTE
Ah, comprendo, indegna moglie, mi vo'
tosto vendicar.

CONTESSA
Mi fa torto quel trasporto; m'oltraggiate a
dubitar.

CONTE
Ah, comprendo, indegna moglie, mi vo'
tosto vendicar.

CONTE
Qua la chiave!

CONTESSA
Egli è innocente...

CONTE
Qua la chiave!

CONTESSA
Egli è innocente. Voi sapete...

CONTE
Non so niente! Va lontan dagli occhi miei,
un'infida, un'empia sei, e mi cerchi
d'infamar!

CONTESSA
Vado...sì...ma...

CONTE
Non ascolto.

COUNTESS
Was to dress him in girl's clothing.

COUNT
Ah, I understand, worthless woman, and I'll
soon get my revenge.

COUNTESS
Your outrage wrongs me, you insult me by
doubting me.

COUNT
Ah, I understand, worthless woman, and I'll
soon get my revenge.

COUNT
Give me the key!

COUNTESS
He is innocent...

COUNT
Give me the key!

COUNTESS
He is innocent, you know it...

COUNT
I know nothing! Get far out of my sight, You
are unfaithful and impious, and you're trying
to humiliate me!

COUNTESS
I'll go, but...

COUNT
I won't listen.

CONTESSA
ma...

CONTE
non ascolto.

CONTESSA *(dà la chieve al Conte)*
...non son rea!

CONTE
Vel leggo in volto! Mora, mora, più non sia
ria cagion del mio penar.

CONTESSA
Ah! La cieca gelosia, quale eccesso gli fa far!

COUNTESS
but...

COUNT
I won't listen.

COUNTESS *(giving him the key)*
I am not guilty!

COUNT
I read it in your face! He shall die and be
no longer the source of my troubles.

COUNTESS
Ah! Blind jealousy, what excesses you bring
about!

(The Count unsheathes his sword and opens the closet door. Susanna comes out)

CONTE
Susanna!

CONTESSA
Susanna!

SUSANNA
Sgnore! Cos'è quel stupore? Il brando prendete, il paggio uccidete, quel paggio malnato vedetelo qua.

CONTE
Che scola! La testa girando mi va!

CONTESSA
Che storia è mai questa, Susanna v'è là!

COUNT
Susanna!

COUNTESS
Susanna!

SUSANNA
Sir! What is this amazement? Take your
sword and kill the page, that low-born
page, you see before you.

COUNT
A revelation! I feel my head spinning!

COUNTESS
What a strange tale, Susanna was in there!

SUSANNA
Confusa han la testa, non san come va!

SUSANNA
Their heads are muddled. They don't know what happened!

CONTE *(a Susanna)*
Sei sola?

COUNT *(to Susanna)*
Are you alone?

SUSANNA
Guardate, qui ascoso sarà.

SUSANNA
See yourself whether anyone is in there.

CONTE
Guardiamo, qui ascoso sarà, ecc.

COUNT
We'll look, someone could be in there, etc.

(he goes into the dressing room)

CONTESSA
Susanna, son morta...il fiato mi manca.

COUNTESS
Susanna, I'm finished, I cannot breathe.

SUSANNA
Più lieta, più franca, in salvo è di già.

SUSANNA
Softly, don't worry, he's already safe.

CONTE *(escendo confuso dal gabinetto)*
Che sbaglio mai presi! Appena lo credo; se a torto v'offesi perdono vi chiedo, ma far burla simile è poi crudeltà.

COUNT *(emerging from the dressing room in confusion)*
What an error I made! I hardly believe it; if I've done you wrong, I beg your pardon, but playing such jokes is cruel, after all.

CONTESSA, SUSANNA
Le vostre follie non mertan pietà.

COUNTESS, SUSANNA
Your foolish acts deserve no pity.

CONTE
Io v'amo!

COUNT
I love you!

CONTESSA
Nol dite!

COUNTESS
Don't say it!

CONTE
Vel giuro!

COUNT
I swear!

CONTESSA
Mentite! Son l'empia, l'infida ch'ognora v'inganna.

CONTE
Quell'ira, Susanna, m'aita a calmar.

SUSANNA
Così si condanna chi può sospettar.

CONTESSA
Adunque la fede d'un'anima amante, sì fiera mercede doveva sperar?

CONTE
Quell'ira, Susanna, ecc.

SUSANNA
Così si condanno, ecc. Signora!

CONTE
Rosina!

CONTESSA
Crudele! Più quella non sono! Ma il misero oggetto del vostro abbandono che avete diletto di far disperar. Crudele, crudele! Soffrir sì gran torto quest'alma non sa.

CONTE
Confuso, pentito, son troppo punito; abbiate pietà.

SUSANNA
Confuso, pentito, è troppo punito; abbiate pietà.

COUNTESS
You're lying. I'm unfaithful and impious, and trying to humiliate you.

COUNT
Help me, Susanna, to calm her anger.

SUSANNA
Thus are condemned the suspicious.

COUNTESS
Should then a faithful lover's soul expect in return such harsh thanks?

COUNT
Help me, Susanna, etc.

SUSANNA
Thus are condemned, etc. My lady!

COUNT
Rosina!

COUNTESS
Cruel man! I am now no more than the miserable object of your desertion, whom you delight in driving to despair. Cruel, cruel man! This soul cannot bear to suffer such wrong.

COUNT
Confused, repentant, I've been punished enough; have pity on me.

SUSANNA
Confused, repentant, he's been punished enough; have pity on him.

CONTE
Ma il paggio rinchiuso?

CONTESSA
Fu sol per provarvi.

CONTE
Ma il tremiti, i palpiti?

CONTESSA
Fu sol per burlarvi.

CONTE
E un foglio sì barbaro?

SUSANNA, CONTESSA
Di Figaro è il foglio, e a voi per Basilio...

CONTE
Ah, perfidi...io voglio...

SUSANNA, CONTESSA
Perdono non merta chi agli altri non dà.

CONTE
Ebben, se vi piace, comune è la pace; Rosina inflessibile con me non sarà.

CONTESSA
Ah quanto, Susanna, son dolce di core! Di donne al furore chi più crederà?

SUSANNA
Cogli uomin, signora, girate, volgete, vedrete che ognora si cade poi là.

COUNT
But the page locked inside?

COUNTESS
Was only to test you.

COUNT
But the trembling, the excitement?

COUNTESS
Was only to ridicule you.

COUNT
And that wretched letter?

SUSANNA, COUNTESS
The letter is from Figaro and for you through Basilio.

COUNT
Ah, tricksters! If I could...

SUSANNA, COUNTESS
He deserves no pardon who withholds it from others.

COUNT
Well, if you please, let us make peace; Rosina will not be unforgiving with me.

COUNTESS
Ah, Susanna, how soft I am in the heart! Who would believe again in woman's anger?

SUSANNA
With men, my lady, we must hesitate and falter, you see how honour soon falls before them.

CONTE
Guardatemi!

CONTESSA
Ingrato!

CONTE
Guardatemi!

CONTESSA
Ingrato!

CONTE
Guardatemi, ho torto, e mi pento.

SUSANNA, CONTESSA, CONTE
Da questo momento quest'alma a conoscerla/mi/vi apprender potrà, ecc.

(Figaro enters)

FIGARO
Signori, di fuori son già i suonatori, le trombe sentite, i pifferi udite, tra canti, tra balli de' vostri vassalli, corriamo, voliamo le nozze a compir.

CONTE
Pian piano, men fretta...

FIGARO
La turba m'aspetta.

CONTE
Pian piano, men fretta, un dubbio toglietemi in pria di partir.

COUNT
Look at me!

COUNTESS
Ungrateful.

COUNT
Look at me!

COUNTESS
Ungrateful!

COUNT
Look at me! I was wrong and I repent!

SUSANNA, COUNTESS, COUNT
From this moment on he/I/you will try to learn to understand each other, etc.

FIGARO
My lords, the musicians are already outside. Hear the trumpets, and listen to the pipes. With singing and dancing for all the peasants...let's hurry out to perform the wedding!

COUNT
Calm down, less haste.

FIGARO
The crowd is waiting.

COUNT
Calm down, less haste, relieve me of a doubt before you go.

SUSANNA, CONTESSA, FIGARO
La cosa è scabrosa, com ha da finir, ecc.

CONTE
Con arte le carte convien qui scoprir, ecc.

CONTE
Conoscete, signor Figaro, questo foglio chi
vergò?

(he shows him a letter)

FIGARO
Nol conosco!

SUSANNA
Nol conosci?

FIGARO
No!

CONTESSA
Nol conosci?

FIGARO
No!

CONTE
Nol conosci?

FIGARO
No!

SUSANNA, CONTESSA, CONTE
Nol conosci?

SUSANNA, COUNTESS, FIGARO
A nasty situation; how will it all end? etc.

COUNT
Now I must play my cards carefully, etc.

COUNT
Do you know, my good Figaro, who wrote
this letter?

FIGARO
I don't know.

SUSANNA
You don't know?

FIGARO
No.

COUNTESS
You don't know?

FIGARO
No.

COUNT
You don't know?

FIGARO
No.

SUSANNA, COUNTESS, COUNT
You don't know?

FIGARO
No, no, no!

SUSANNA
E nol desti a Don Basilio?

CONTESSA
Per recarlo...

CONTE
Tu c'intendi?

FIGARO
Oibò, oibò!

SUSANNA
E non sai del damerino...

CONTESSA
Che stasera nel giardino...

CONTE
Già capisci?

FIGARO
Io non lo so.

CONTE
Cerchi invan difesa e scusa, il tuo ceffo già t'accusa, vedo ben che vuoi mentir.

FIGARO
Mente il ceffo, io già non mento.

SUSANNA, CONTESSA
Il talento aguzzi invano, palesato abbiam l'arcano, non v'è nulla da ridir.

FIGARO
No, no, no.

SUSANNA
Didn't you give it to Don Basilio?

COUNTESS
To take it...

COUNT
Do you understand?

FIGARO
Alas, alas!

SUSANNA
And don't you remember the young fop?

COUNTESS
who tonight in the garden...

COUNT
Now you understand?

FIGARO
I don't know.

COUNT
In vain you look for defences, excuses, your own face accuses you; I see very well you're lying.

FIGARO
My face may be lying, but not I.

SUSANNA, COUNTESS
You've sharpened your wits in vain; the whole secret is out, and there's no use complaining.

CONTE
Che rispondi?

FIGARO
Niente, niente!

CONTE
Dunque accordi?

FIGARO
Non accordo!

SUSANNA, CONTESSA
Eh via chetati, balordo, la burletta ha da finir.

FIGARO
Per finirla lietamente, e all'usanza teatrale, un'azion matrimoniale la faremo ora seguir.

SUSANNA, CONTESSA, FIGARO
Deh signor, nol contrastate, consolate i miei/lor desir.

CONTE
Marcellina! Marcellina! Quanto tardi a comparir! ecc.

COUNT
What's your answer?

FIGARO
Simply nothing.

COUNT
Then you admit it?

FIGARO
I do not!

SUSANNA, COUNTESS
Go on, keep quiet, you fool, the little game is over.

FIGARO
To give it a happy ending as is usual in the theatre, we'll proceed now to a matrimonial tableau.

SUSANNA, COUNTESS, FIGARO
Come sir, don't be obstinate; give in to my/their wishes.

COUNT
Marcellina, Marcellina, how long you delay in coming! etc.

(Antonio comes in, rather drunk, holding a pot of crushed carnations)

ANTONIO
Ah! Signor, signor!

CONTE
Cosa è stato?

ANTONIO
Ah! Sir, sir!

COUNT
What has happened?

ANTONIO
Che insolenza! Chi'l fece? Chi fu?

SUSANNA, CONTESSA, CONTE, FIGARO
Cosa dici, cos'hai, cosa è nato?

ANTONIO
Ascoltate!

SUSANNA, CONTESSA, CONTE, FIGARO
Via parla, di' su!

ANTONIO
Ascoltate! Dal balcone che guarda in giardino mille cose ogni dì gittar veggio, e
poc'anzi, può darsi di peggio, vidi un uom,
signor mio, gittar giù.

CONTE
Dal balcone?

ANTONIO (*additandogli i fiori*)
Vedete i garofani,

CONTE
In giardino?

ANTONIO
Sì!

SUSANNA, CONTESSA (*sotto voce*)
Figaro, all'erta!

CONTE
Cosa sento?

ANTONIO
What insolence! Who did it? Who?

SUSANNA, COUNTESS, COUNT, FIGARO
What are you saying, what's this, what is it?

ANTONIO
Listen to me!

SUSANNA, COUNTESS, COUNT, FIGARO
Go ahead, speak up!

ANTONIO
Listen to me! From the balcony that looks
out on the garden I've seen a thousand things
thrown down; but just now, what could be
worse? I saw a man, my lord, thrown out!

COUNT
From the balcony?

ANTONIO (*showing the pot*)
See these carnations!

COUNT
Into the garden?

ANTONIO
Yes!

SUSANNA, COUNTESS (*quietly*)
Figaro, get ready!

COUNT
What's this I hear?

SUSANNA, CONTESSA, FIGARO
Costui ci sconcerta, quel briaco che viene a far qui?

CONTE *(ad Antonio)*
Dunque un uom, ma dov'è gito?

ANTONIO
Ratto, ratto, il birbone è fuggito, e ad un tratto di vista m'uscì.

SUSANNA *(a Figaro)*
Sai che il paggio...

FIGARO *(a Susanna)*
So tutto, lo vidi.

(laughing loudly)

Ah ah ah ah!

CONTE
Taci là!

FIGARO
Ah ah ah ah!

ANTONIO
Cosa ridi?

FIGARO
Ah ah ah ah! Tu sei cotto dal sorger del dì.

CONTE *(ad Antonio)*
Or ripetimi, ripetimi: un uom dal balcone?

SUSANNA, COUNTESS, FIGARO
The fellow has upset everything; What is that drunkard doing here?

COUNT *(to Antonio)*
That man, where did he land?

ANTONIO
Quick as a flash, the scoundrel fled right away out of my sight!

SUSANNA *(to Figaro)*
You know, the page...

FIGARO *(to Susanna)*
I know everything, I saw him.

Ha ha ha ha!

COUNT
Be quiet over there!

FIGARO
Ha ha ha ha!

ANTONIO
Why are you laughing?

FIGARO
Ha ha ha ha. You're tipsy from break of day.

COUNT *(to Antonio)*
Tell me again, a man from the balcony?

ANTONIO
Dal balcone.

CONTE
In giardino?

ANTONIO
In giardino.

SUSANNA, CONTESSA, FIGARO
Ma signore, se in lui parla il vino.

CONTE
Segui pure; né in volto il vedesti?

ANTONIO
No, nol vidi.

SUSANNA, CONTESSA
Olà, Figaro, ascolta!

CONTE
Sì?

ANTONIO
Nol vidi.

FIGARO
Vidi piangione, sta' zitto una volta! Per tre soldi da fare un tumulto: giacché il fatto non può stare occulto, sono io stesso salta-to di lì!

CONTE
Chi! Voi stesso?

SUSANNA, CONTESSA
Che testa! Che ingegno!

ANTONIO
From the balcony.

COUNT
Into the garden?

ANTONIO
Into the garden.

SUSANNA, COUNTESS, FIGARO
But sir, it's the wine talking!

COUNT
Go on anyway; you didn't see his face?

ANTONIO
No, I didn't.

SUSANNA, COUNTESS
Hey, Figaro, listen!

COUNT
Yes?

ANTONIO
I didn't see him.

FIGARO
Go on, old blubberer, be quiet for once. Making such a fuss for threepence! Since the fact can't be kept quiet, it was I who jumped from there!

COUNT
You? Yourself?

SUSANNA, COUNTESS
What a brain! A genius!

FIGARO
Che stupor!

ANTONIO
Chi! Voi stesso?

SUSANNA, CONTESSA
Che testa! Che ingegno!

FIGARO
Che stupor!

CONTE
Già creder nol posso.

ANTONIO *(a Figaro)*
Come mai diventasti sì grosso? Dopo il salto non fosti così.

FIGARO
A chi salta succede così.

ANTONIO
Ch'il direbbe?

SUSANNA, CONTESSA *(a Figaro)*
Ed insiste quel pazzo?

CONTE *(ad Antonio)*
Tu che dici?

ANTONIO
A me parve il ragazzo...

CONTE
Cherubin!

FIGARO
What an upset!

ANTONIO
You? Yourself?

SUSANNA, COUNTESS
What a brain! A genius!

FIGARO
What an upset!

COUNT
I cannot believe it.

ANTONIO *(to Figaro)*
When did you grow so big? When you jumped you weren't like that.

FIGARO
That's how people look when they jump.

ANTONIO
Who says so?

SUSANNA, COUNTESS *(to Figaro)*
Is the fool being stubborn?

COUNT *(to Antonio)*
What are you saying?

ANTONIO
To me it looked like the boy.

COUNT
Cherubino!

SUSANNA, CONTESSA
Maledetto! Maledetto!

FIGARO
Esso appunto, da Siviglia a cavallo qui giunto, da Siviglia ove forse sarà.

ANTONIO
Questo no; che il cavallo io non vidi saltare di là.

CONTE
Che pazienza! Finiam questo ballo!

SUSANNA, CONTESSA
Come mai, giusto ciel, finirà?

CONTE
Dunque tu?

FIGARO
Saltai giù...

CONTE
Ma perché?

FIGARO
Il timor...

CONTE
Che timor...?

FIGARO
Là rinchiuso, aspettando quel caro viset-to...tippe, tappe un sussurro fuor d'uso voi gridaste... lo scritto biglietto... saltai giù dal terrore confuso, e stravolto m'ho un nervo del piè.

SUSANNA, COUNTESS
Damn you!

FIGARO
At this moment he must be on horseback, arriving at Seville.

ANTONIO
No, that's not so; I saw no horse when he jumped out of the window.

COUNT
Patience! Let's wind up this nonsense!

SUSANNA, COUNTESS
How, in the name of Heaven, will it end?

COUNT
So then you...

FIGARO
Jumped down.

COUNT
But why?

FIGARO
Out of fear...

COUNT
What...fear?

FIGARO
Here inside I was waiting for that dear face...When I heard an unusual noise...you were shouting...I thought of the letter...and jumped out confused by fear, and pulled the muscles in my ankle!

ANTONIO *(mostrando una carta)*
Vostre dunque saran queste carte che perdeste...

CONTE *(cogliendole)*
Olà, porgile a me!

FIGARO
Sono in trappola.

SUSANNA, CONTESSA
Figaro, all'erta.

CONTE *(apre il foglio poi lo chiude tosto)*
Dite un po', questo foglio cos'è?

FIGARO *(cava di tasca alcune carte e finge di guardarle)*
Tosto, tosto ne ho tanti, aspettate!

ANTONIO
Sarà forse il sommario dei debiti?

FIGARO
No, la lista degli osti.

CONTE *(a Figaro)*
Parlate?

(to Antonio)

E tu lascialo.

SUSANNA, CONTESSA, FIGARO
(ad Antonio)
Lascialo/mi, e parti.

ANTONIO *(showing the page's papers)*
Then these papers must be yours, and you lost them?

COUNT *(seizing them)*
Here, give them to me.

FIGARO
I am in a trap.

SUSANNA, COUNTESS
Figaro, get ready.

COUNT *(quickly glancing at the papers)*
Tell me now, what letter is this?

FIGARO *(taking some papers from his pocket and looking at them)*
Wait, I have so many...just a moment.

ANTONIO
Perhaps it is a list of your debts.

FIGARO
No, the list of innkeepers.

COUNT *(to Figaro)*
Speak.

You leave him alone.

SUSANNA, COUNTESS, FIGARO
(to Antonio)
Leave/him/me alone, and get out.

ANTONIO
Parto sì, ma se tomo a trovarti...

SUSANNA, CONTESSA, CONTE
Lascialo.

FIGARO
Vanne, vanne, non temo di te.

SUSANNA, CONTESSA, CONTE
Lascialo.

ANTONIO
Parto sì, ecc.

FIGARO
Vanne, vanne, non temo di te.

SUSANNA, CONTESSA, CONTE
Lascialo, e parti.

(Antonio leaves)

CONTE *(il foglio in man)*
Dunque?

CONTESSA *(piano a Susanna)*
O ciel! La patente del paggio!

SUSANNA *(piano a Figaro)*
Giusti dei! La patente!

CONTE
Coraggio!

FIGARO
Ah che testa! Quest'è la patente che
poc'anzi il fanciullo mi diè.

ANTONIO
I'm leaving, but if I catch you once more...

SUSANNA, COUNTESS, COUNT
Leave him alone.

FIGARO
Get out, I'm not afraid of you.

SUSANNA, COUNTESS, COUNT
Leave him alone.

ANTONIO
I'm leaving, etc.

FIGARO
Get out, I'm not afraid of you.

SUSANNA, COUNTESS, COUNT
Leave him alone, and get out.

COUNT *(opening the papers)*
Well now?

COUNTESS *(softly to Susanna)*
Heavens! The page's commission!

SUSANNA *(softly to Figaro)*
Ye gods! The commission!

COUNT
Speak up!

FIGARO
Oh, what a brain! It's the commission that
the boy gave me a while ago.

CONTE
Perché fare?

FIGARO
Vi manca...

CONTE
Vi manca?

CONTESSA *(piano a Susanna)*
Il suggello!

SUSANNA *(piano a Figaro)*
Il suggello!

CONTE
Rispondi!

FIGARO *(fingendo d'esitare ancora)*
È l'usanza...

CONTE
Su via, ti confondi?

FIGARO
È l'usanza di porvi il suggello.

CONTE
Questo birbo mi toglie il cervello, tutto è
un mistero per me, sì, ecc.

SUSANNA, CONTESSA
Se mi salvo da questa tempesta, più non
avvi naufragio per me, no, ecc.

FIGARO
Sbuffa invano e la terra calpesta! Poverino
ne sa men di me, ecc.

COUNT
What for?

FIGARO
It needs...

COUNT
It needs...?

COUNTESS *(softly to Susanna)*
The seal!

SUSANNA *(softly to Figaro)*
The seal!

COUNT
Your answer?

FIGARO *(pretending to think)*
It's the custom...

COUNT
Come on now, are you confused?

FIGARO
It's the custom to place a seal on it.

COUNT
This rascal drives me crazy; the whole
thing's a mystery to me.

SUSANNA, COUNTESS
If I survive this tempest I won't be ship-
wrecked after all, etc.

FIGARO
He pants and paws the ground in vain.
Poor man, he knows less than I do, etc.

(Marcellina, Bartolo and Basilio enter)

MARCELLINA, BASILIO, BARTOLO
Voi signor, che giusto siete, ci dovete or ascoltar.

SUSANNA, CONTESSA, FIGARO
Son venuti a sconcertarmi qual rimedio a ritrovar?

CONTE
Son venuti a vendicarmi, io mi sento a consolar.

FIGARO
Son tre stolidi, tre pazzi, cosa mai vengono da far?

CONTE
Pian pianin senza schiamazzi, dica ognun quel che gli par.

MARCELLINA
Un impegno nuziale ha costui con me contratto, e pretendo ch'il contratto deva meco effettuar.

SUSANNA, CONTESSA, FIGARO
Come? Come?

CONTE
Olà! Silenzio! Io son qui per giudicar.

BARTOLO
Io da lei scelto avvocato vengo a far le sue difese, le legittime pretese io vi vengo a palesar.

MARCELLINA, BASILIO, BARTOLO
You, sir, who are so just, you must listen to us now.

SUSANNA, COUNTESS, FIGARO
They have come to ruin me what solution can I find?

COUNT
They have come to avenge me. I'm beginning to feel better.

FIGARO
They are all three stupid fools, whatever they have come to do?

COUNT
Softly now, without this clamour, let everyone speak his mind.

MARCELLINA
That man has signed a contract binding him to marry me, and I contend that the contract must be carried out.

SUSANNA, COUNTESS, FIGARO
What, what?

COUNT
Hey, be silent! I am here to render judgment.

BARTOLO
Appointed as her lawyer I am here in her defense, to publish to the world her legitimate reasons.

SUSANNA, CONTESSA, FIGARO
È un birbante!

CONTE
Olà! Silenzio! ecc.

BASILIO
Io com' uomo al mondo cognito, vengo
qui per testimonio del promesso matrimonio con prestanza di danar.

SUSANNA, CONTESSA, FIGARO
Son tre matti, ecc.

CONTE
Olà! Silenzio! Lo vedremo, il contratto leg-
geremo, tutto in ordin deve andar.

SUSANNA, CONTESSA, FIGARO
Son confusa(o), son stordita(o)
disperata(o), sbalordita(o)! Certo un diavol
dell'inferno qui li/ci ha fatti capitar!

**MARCELLINA, BASILIO, BARTOLO,
CONTE**
Che bel colpo! Che bel caso! È cresciuto a
tutti il naso; qualche nume a noi propizio,
qui ci/li ha fatti capitar!

SUSANNA, COUNTESS, FIGARO
He is a rogue!

COUNT
Hey, be silent! etc.

BASILIO
Know as a man of the world, I come here
as a witness of his promise of marriage
when she loaned him some money.

SUSANNA, COUNTESS, FIGARO
They are all mad, etc.

COUNT
Hey, be silent; we'll see about that. We will
read the contract and proceed in due order.

SUSANNA, COUNTESS, FIGARO
I am confused, stupefied, hopeless, dis-
mayed! Surely some devil from Hell has
brought them/us here!

**MARCELLINA, BASILIO, BARTOLO,
COUNT**
A telling blow, a lucky chance! Victory is
right before our noses; some propitious
power has surely brought them/us here!

Act 3

A salon in the castle

(The salon is decorated for a wedding feast. The Count is alone, pacing up and down)

Recitative

CONTE	COUNT
Che imbarazzo è mai questo! Un foglio anonimo... la cameriera in gabinetto chiusa... la padrona confusa... un uom che salta dal balcone in giardino, un altro appresso, che dice esser quel desso... Non so cosa pensar, potrebbe forse qualcun de' miei vassalli... a simil razza è comune l'ardir, ma la Contessa... ah che un dubbio l'offende! Ella rispetta troppo sé stessa, e l'onor mio... l'onore... dove diamin l'ha posto umano errore!	Why, what kind of embarrassing situation is this? An anonymous letter, the maid shut up in the closet, her mistress, confused, a man who jumps from balcony to garden, then another who says it was he who jumped. I don't know what to think. It could be that one of my vassals...people of their class often grow bold...But the Countess? Ah, how suspicion offends her! She has too high respect for herself and for my honour...honour...where the devil has human error placed it!

(The Countess and Susanna appear at the back)

CONTESSA	COUNTESS
Via! Fatti core, digli che ti attenda in giardino.	Go ahead: take heart, and tell him that you'll wait for him in the garden.

CONTE
Saprò se Cherubino era giunto a Siviglia, a
tale oggetto ho mandato Basilio.

SUSANNA
O cielo! E Figaro?

CONTESSA
A lui non dei dir nulla, in vece tua voglio
andarci io medesma.

CONTE
Avanti sera dovrebbe ritornar.

SUSANNA
Oh Dio! Non oso.

CONTESSA
Pensa ch'è in tua mano il mio riposo.

(she leaves)

CONTE
E Susanna? Chi sa, ch'ella tradito abbia il
segreto mio... oh, se ha parlato, gli fo'
sposar la vecchia.

SUSANNA
(Marcellina...)
Signor!

CONTE
Cosa bramate?

SUSANNA
Mi par che siate in collera!

COUNT
I'll find out whether Cherubino reached
Seville; for that purpose I've sent Basilio.

SUSANNA
Heavens! What about Figaro?

COUNTESS
Say nothing to him. I'll go to see him
myself.

COUNT
He should return this evening.

SUSANNA
O God! I dare not.

COUNTESS
Consider that in your hands lies my peace.

COUNT
And Susanna? Who knows, perhaps she
betrayed my secret; oh, if she has told, I'll
make him marry the old woman.

SUSANNA
(Marcellina...)
Sir!

COUNT
What do you want?

SUSANNA
It seems to me you're angry.

CONTE
Volete qualche cosa?

SUSANNA
Signor, la vostra sposa ha i soliti vapori, e vi chiede il fiaschetto degli odori.

CONTE
Prendete.

SUSANNA
Or vel riporto.

CONTE
Ah no; potete ritenerlo per voi.

SUSANNA
Per me? Questi non son mali da donne triviali.

CONTE
Un' amante che perde il caro sposo sul punto d'ottenerlo?

SUSANNA
Pagando Marcellina colla dote che voi mi prometteste...

CONTE
Ch'io vi promisi! Quando?

SUSANNA
Credea d'averlo inteso...

CONTE
Sì, se voluto aveste intendermi voi stessa.

COUNT
Do you desire something?

SUSANNA
Sir, your wife is having her vapours, and asks you for her little smelling bottle.

COUNT
Take it.

SUSANNA
I'll bring it back.

COUNT
Ah no, you may keep it for yourself.

SUSANNA
For myself? That is no affliction for women of my class.

COUNT
Not even for a lover who loses her dear husband on the verge of getting him?

SUSANNA
By paying Marcellina with the dowry that you promised me...

COUNT
That I promised you? When?

SUSANNA
I believe that it was understood.

COUNT
Yes, if you had been disposed to understand me yourself.

SUSANNA
È mio dovere, e quel di Sua Eccellenza è il mio volere.

SUSANNA
Such is my duty, and my wish is that of Your Excellency.

disc no. 2/track 2 *No. 16: Duetto* In this "duetto," the Count nervously asks Susanna if she'll meet him in the garden that evening, and she assures him—letting us know that she's lying—that she will. The rhythm and highly expressive, if simple, vocal lines find the Count practically begging—how his lust has brought him down!!—and Susanna playing with him exquisitely.

CONTE
Crudel! Perchè finora farmi languir così?

COUNT
Heartless! Why until now did you leave me to languish?

SUSANNA
Signor, la donna ognora tempo ha di dir di sì.

SUSANNA
Sir, every lady has here time to say yes.

CONTE
Dunque in giardin verrai?

COUNT
Then you'll come to the garden?

SUSANNA
Se piace a voi, verrò.

SUSANNA
If it pleases you, I'll come.

CONTE
E non mi mancherai?

COUNT
And you won't fail me?

SUSANNA
No, non vi mancherò.

SUSANNA
No, I won't fail you.

CONTE
Verrai?

COUNT
You'll come?

SUSANNA
Sì.

SUSANNA
Yes.

CONTE
Non mancherai?

COUNT
You won't fail me?

SUSANNA
No.

CONTE
Non mancherai?

SUSANNA
No, non vi mancherò.

CONTE
Mi sento dal contento pieno di gioia il cor!

SUSANNA
Scusatemi se mento, voi ch'intendete amor!

CONTE
Dunque in giardin verrai?

SUSANNA
Se piace a voi, verrò.

CONTE
E non mi mancherai?

SUSANNA
No, non vi mancherò.

CONTE
Verrai?

SUSANNA
Sì.

CONTE
Non mancherai?

SUSANNA
No.

COUNT
You won't fail me?

SUSANNA
No, I won't fail you.

COUNT
My contented heart now feels full of joy!

SUSANNA
Forgive me if I am lying all you who
understand love's ways!

COUNT
Then you'll come to the garden?

SUSANNA
If it pleases you, I'll come.

COUNT
And you won't fail me?

SUSANNA
No, I won't fail you.

COUNT
You'll come?

SUSANNA
Yes.

COUNT
You won't fail me?

SUSANNA
No.

CONTE
Dunque verrai?

SUSANNA
No!

CONTE
No?

SUSANNA
Sì, se piace a voi, verrò.

CONTE
Non mancherai?

SUSANNA
No!

CONTE
Dunque verrai?

SUSANNA
Sì!

CONTE
Non mancherai?

SUSANNA
Sì!

CONTE
Sì?

SUSANNA
No, non vi macherò.

SUSANNA
No.

COUNT
So you'll come?

SUSANNA
No!

COUNT
No?

SUSANNA
I mean, yes, if you wish it.

COUNT
You'll not fail me?

SUSANNA
No!

COUNT
So you'll come?

SUSANNA
Yes!

COUNT
You'll not fail me?

SUSANNA
Yes!

COUNT
Yes?

SUSANNA
I mean, no, I'll not fail you.

CONTE
Mi sento dal contento, ecc.

SUSANNA
Scusatemi se mento, ecc.

Recitative

CONTE
E perchè fosti meco stamattina si austera?

SUSANNA
Col paggio ch'ivi c'era.

CONTE
Ed a Basilio, che per me ti parlò?

SUSANNA
Ma qual bisogno abbiam noi, che un Basilio...

CONTE
È vero, è vero, e mi prometti poi... se tu manchi, oh cor mio... ma la Contessa attenderà il vasetto.

SUSANNA
Eh, fu un pretesto, parlato io non avrei senza di questo.

CONTE
Carissima!

SUSANNA
Vien gente.

COUNT
My contented heart, etc.

SUSANNA
Forgive me if I am lying, etc.

COUNT
And why were you so austere with me this morning?

SUSANNA
Because the page was with us.

COUNT
And with Basilio, who spoke with you for me?

SUSANNA
Why, what need have we of a Basilio?

COUNT
That's true, true; so you promise me then... if you fail me, my heart...But the Countess must be waiting for the little bottle.

SUSANNA
Oh, that was only an excuse, I wouldn't have dared to speak without one.

COUNT
Dearest!

SUSANNA
Someone's coming.

CONTE *(tra sé)*
È mia senz'altro.

SUSANNA *(tra sé)*
Forbitevi la bocca, o signor scaltro.

(enter Figaro)

FIGARO
Ehi, Susanna, ove vai?

SUSANNA
Taci: senza avvocato hai già vinta la causa.

FIGARO
Cos'è nato?

(they go out together)

COUNT *(aside)*
She's mine, for sure.

SUSANNA *(to herself)*
Sharpen up your tongue, crafty sir.

FIGARO
Hey, Susanna, where are you going?

SUSANNA
Hush! Without a lawyer our case is won already!

FIGARO
What's happened?

disc no. 2/track 4 *No. 17: Recitative and Aria* It is here that the Count finally realizes that he has lost control of the goings-on in his palace, and his rage is palpable. The recitative is written in short phrases since so much is going through the Count's mind, and Mozart lets us feel how disjointed it is to the Count by not giving us a melody to latch on to. It is not surprising that the aria proper is so difficult to sing—with octave leaps, drastic dynamic changes, maddening coloratura and a devilish trill—the Count is mad with fury. All decorum is lost—this man is hanging on by a thread.

CONTE
Hai già vinta la causa! Cosa sento! In qual laccio cadea? Perfidi. Io voglio... io voglio di tal modo punirvi, a piacer mio la sentenza sarà... Ma se pagasse le vecchia pretendente? Pagarla! In qual maniera? E poi v'è Antonio che all'incognito Figaro ricusa

COUNT
Their case is won! What's that! What trap have I fallen into? Tricksters! I'm going to...I'm going to punish you in such a way...the punishment shall be what I choose...But what if he should pay the old suitor? Pay her! With what? And then there

di dare una nipote in matrimonio. Coltivando l'orgoglio di questo mentecatto... tutto giova a un raggiro... il colpo è fatto. Vedrò, mentr'io sospiro, felice un servo mio! E un ben che invan desio, ei posseder dovrà? Vedrò per man d'amore unita a un vile oggetto chi in me destò un affetto che per me poi non ha? Vedrò mentr'io sospiro, ecc. Ah no, lasciarti in pace, non vo questo contento, tu non nascesti, audace, per dare a me tormento, e forse ancor per ridere, di mia infelicità! Già la speranza sola delle vendette mie quest'anima consola, e giubilar mi fa! Ah, che lasciarti in pace, ecc.

is Antonio, who will refuse to give his niece in marriage to the upstart Figaro. By flattering the pride of that half-wit...Everything's falling into my scheme...I'll strike while the iron's hot. Shall I live to see a servant of mine happy and enjoying pleasure that I desire in vain? Shall I see the hand of love unite a lowly person to one who arouses feelings in me she does not feel herself? Shall I live to see, etc. Ah no! I shall not leave that carefree creature in peace; you were not born, bold fellow, to give me torment or perhaps to laugh at my unhappiness. Now only hope of my revenge consoles my soul and makes me rejoice! Ah. I shall not leave, etc.

(enter Marcellina, Don Curzio, Figaro, Bartolo)

CURZIO
E' decisa la lite. O pagarla, o sposarla. Ora ammutite.

CURZIO
The case is settled. Either pay her, or marry her. Now be silent.

MARCELLINA
Io respiro.

MARCELLINA
I breathe again.

FIGARO
Ed io moro.

FIGARO
And I die.

MARCELLINA *(tra sé)*
Alfin sposa sarò d'un uom ch'adoro.

MARCELLINA *(to herself)*
At last I shall marry the man I adore.

FIGARO
Eccellenza! M'appello...

FIGARO
Your Excellency! I appeal...

CONTE
È giusta la sentenza, o pagar, o sposar—
bravo, Don Curzio.

CURZIO
Bontà di Sua Eccellenza.

BARTOLO
Che superba sentenza!

FIGARO
In che superba?

BARTOLO
Siam tutti vendicatti...

FIGARO
Io non la sposerò.

BARTOLO
La sposerai.

CURZIO
O pagarla, o sposarla.

MARCELLINA
Io t'ho prestati due mila pezzi duri.

FIGARO
Son gentiluomo, e senza l'assenso de' miei
nobili parenti...

CONTE
Dove sono? Chi sono?

FIGARO
Lasciate ancor cercarli: dopo dieci anni io
spero di trovarli.

COUNT
The sentence is just. Either pay or marry—
bravo, Don Curzio!

CURZIO
Your Excellency is too good!

BARTOLO
What a perfect sentence!

FIGARO
How do you mean, perfect?

BARTOLO
We are all avenged...

FIGARO
I won't marry her.

BARTOLO
You will marry her.

CURZIO
Either pay her or marry her.

MARCELLINA
I lent you two thousand silver crowns.

FIGARO
I am a gentleman, and without the consent
of my noble parents...

COUNT
Where are they? Who are they?

FIGARO
Let them be searched for again; for ten
years I've been trying to find them.

BARTOLO
Qualche bambin trovato?

FIGARO
No, perduto, dottor, anzi rubato.

CONTE
Come?

MARCELLINA
Cosa?

BARTOLO
La prova?

CURZIO
Il testimonio?

FIGARO
L'oro, le gemme e i ricamati panni, che ne'
più teneri anni mi ritrovaron addosso i
masnadieri, sono gl'indizi veri di mia nasci-
ta illustre, e soprattutto questo al mio braccio impresso geroglifico.

MARCELLINA
Una spatola impressa al braccio destro?

FIGARO
E a voi ch'il disse?

MARCELLINA
Oh Dio! È desso!

FIGARO
È ver, son io.

BARTOLO
A foundling child?

FIGARO
No a lost child, doctor, or rather, kidnapped...

COUNT
How's that?

MARCELLINA
What?

BARTOLO
Your proof?

CURZIO
Your witnesses?

FIGARO
The gold, gems and embroidered clothes
that the robbers found me wearing even at
that tender age are the true indications of
my high birth, and especially this hiero-
glyphic on my arm.

MARCELLINA
A spatula birthmark on your right arm?

FIGARO
And who was it told you?

MARCELLINA
Oh God! It is he!

FIGARO
Of course, I am he.

CURZIO Chi?	**CURZIO** Who?
CONTE Chi?	**COUNT** Who?
BARTOLO Chi?	**BARTOLO** Who?
MARCELLINA Raffaello!	**MARCELLINA** Little Raphael!
BARTOLO E i ladri ti rapir?	**BARTOLO** And the thieves stole you?
FIGARO Presso un castello.	**FIGARO** Near a castle.
BARTOLO Ecco tua madre!	**BARTOLO** There is your mother!
FIGARO Balia...	**FIGARO** My nursemaid?
BARTOLO No, tua madre.	**BARTOLO** No, your mother.
CURZIO, CONTE Sua madre?	**CURZIO, COUNT** His mother?
FIGARO Cosa sento!	**FIGARO** What's this I hear?
MARCELLINA Ecco tuo padre!	**MARCELLINA** There is your father!

No. 18: Sextet If ever comic relief were needed, it is here, and Mozart and da Ponte do not disappoint. With the sudden insight that Figaro is really Marcellina's long-lost son, and even more bizzare—that Bartolo is his father, one entire plot problem (Figaro definitely won't have to marry Marcellina!) is solved and for once, everyone is amazed at the same time. The sudden warmth the three feel towards one another is not allowed any sentimentality—the seemingly endless repitition of "sua madre" and "suo padre" is just too eccentric. This is one of the few moments in all of comic opera which always gets a laugh—both situation and musical treatment are genuinely funny.

(embracing Figaro)
Riconosci in quest'amplesso una madre, amato figlio!

Recognise in this embrace your mother, beloved son.

FIGARO *(a Bartolo)*
Padre mio, fate lo stesso, non mi fate più arrossir.

FIGARO *(to Bartolo)*
My father, do the same, and let me no longer be ashamed.

BARTOLO *(abbracciando Figaro)*
Resistenza, la coscienza far non lascia al tuo desir.

BARTOLO *(embracing Figaro)*
Resistance, my conscience no longer lets you rule.

(Figaro embraces his parents)

CURZIO
Ei suo padre? Ella sua madre? L'imeneo non può seguir.

CURZIO
He's his father? She's his mother? It's too late for the wedding now.

CONTE
Son smarrito, son stordito, meglio è assai di qua partir.

COUNT
I'm astounded, I'm abashed, I'd better get out of here.

MARCELLINA, BARTOLO
Figlio amato!

MARCELLINA, BARTOLO
Beloved son!

FIGARO
Parenti amati!

FIGARO
Beloved parents!

(Susanna enters)

SUSANNA
Alto! Alto! Signor Conte, mille doppie son qui pronte, a pagar vengo per Figaro, ed a porlo in libertà.

MARCELLINA, BARTOLO
Figlio amato!

CURZIO, CONTE
Non sappiam com'è la cosa, osservate un poco là.

FIGARO
Parenti amati!

SUSANNA *(vede Figaro che abbraccia Marcellina)*
Già d'accordo colla sposa, giusti Dei, che infedeltà.

(She wants to leave but Figaro detains her)

Lascia, iniquo!

FIGARO
No, t'arresta! Senti, oh cara, senti!

SUSANNA *(dandogli uno schiaffo)*
Senti questa!

MARCELLINA, BARTOLO, FIGARO
E un effetto di buon core tutto amore è quel che fa, ecc.

SUSANNA *(a parte)*
Fremo, smanio dal furore, una vecchia me la fa, ecc.

SUSANNA
Stop, stop, noble sir, I have a thousand double crowns right here. I come to pay for Figaro and to set him at liberty.

MARCELLINA, BARTOLO
Beloved son!

CURZIO, COUNT
We're not sure what's taking place. Look over there a moment.

FIGARO
Beloved parents!

SUSANNA *(seeing Figaro hugging Marcellina)*
So he's reconciled with his bride; ye gods, what infidelity!

Leave her, villain!

FIGARO
No, wait! Listen, darling

SUSANNA *(boxing Figaro's ears)*
Listen to this!

MARCELLINA, BARTOLO, FIGARO
A natural action of a good heart, pure love is demonstrated here, etc.

SUSANNA *(aside)*
I'm boiling, I'm raging with fury; an old woman has done this to me, etc.

CONTE, CURZIO
Freme/o, e smania/o dal furore, il destino
me la/gliela fa, ecc.

MARCELLINA *(a Susanna)*
Lo sdegno calmate, mia cara figliuola, sua
madre abbracciate che or vostra sarà, ecc.

SUSANNA *(a Bartolo)*
Sua madre?

BARTOLO
Sua madre!

SUSANNA *(al Conte)*
Sua madre?

CONTE
Sua madre!

SUSANNA *(a Curzio)*
Sua madre?

CURZIO
Sua madre!

SUSANNA *(a Marcellina)*
Sua madre?

MARCELLINA
Sua madre!

**MARCELLINA, CURZIO, CONTE,
BARTOLO**
Sua madre!

SUSANNA *(a Figaro)*
Tua madre?

COUNT, CURZIO
He's/I'm boiling, he's/I'm raging with fury;
destiny has done this to me/him. etc.

MARCELLINA *(to Susanna)*
Calm your anger, my dear daughter,
embrace his mother, and yours as well, now.

SUSANNA *(to Bartolo)*
His mother?

BARTOLO
His mother.

SUSANNA *(to the Count)*
His mother?

COUNT
His mother.

SUSANNA *(to Curzio)*
His mother?

CURZIO
His mother.

SUSANNA *(to Marcellina)*
His mother?

MARCELLINA
His mother.

**MARCELLINA, CURZIO, COUNT,
BARTOLO**
His mother!

SUSANNA *(to Figaro)*
Your mother?

FIGARO
E quello è mio padre che a te lo dirà.

SUSANNA *(a Bartolo)*
Suo padre?

BARTOLO
Suo padre!

SUSANNA *(al Conte)*
Suo padre?

CONTE
Suo padre!

SUSANNA *(a Curzio)*
Suo padre?

CURZIO
Suo padre!

SUSANNA *(a Marcellina)*
Suo padre?

MARCELLINA
Suo padre!

MARCELLINA, CURZIO, CONTE, BARTOLO
Suo padre!

SUSANNA *(a Figaro)*
Tuo padre?

FIGARO
E quella è mia madre, che a te lo dirà, ecc.

FIGARO
And that is my father, he'll say so himself.

SUSANNA *(to Bartolo)*
His father?

BARTOLO
His father.

SUSANNA *(to the Count)*
His father?

COUNT
His father.

SUSANNA *(to Curzio)*
His father?

CURZIO
His father.

SUSANNA *(to Marcellina)*
His father?

MARCELLINA
His father.

MARCELLINA, CURZIO, COUNT, BARTOLO
His father!

SUSANNA *(to Figaro)*
Your father?

FIGARO
And that is my mother, who'll say so her-self, etc.

CURZIO, CONTE
Al fiero tormento di questo momento
quest'anima appena resister or sa.

SUSANNA, MARCELLINA, BARTOLO, FIGARO
Al dolce contento di questo momento
quest'anima appena resister or sa.

(the Count leaves with Curzio)

Recitative

MARCELLINA
Eccovi, o caro amico, il dolce frutto del-
l'antico amor nostro.

BARTOLO
Or non parliamo di fatti sì rimoti, egli è
mio figlio, mia consorte voi siete, e le nozze
farem quando volete.

MARCELLINA
Oggi, e doppie saranno;

(to Figaro)

prendi, questo e il biglietto del denar che a
me devi, ed è tua dote.

SUSANNA
Prendi ancor questa borsa.

BARTOLO
E questa ancora.

CURZIO, COUNT
My soul can barely resist any longer the
fierce torture of this moment.

SUSANNA, MARCELLINA, BARTOLO, FIGARO
My soul can barely resist any longer the
sweet delight of this moment.

MARCELLINA
Here you see, dear friend, the sweet fruit of
our ancient love.

BARTOLO
Let us speak no more of such ancient
events; he is my son, you are my wife; we
shall be married whenever you wish.

MARCELLINA
Today, and let it be a double ceremony.

Take this, which is the note for the money
you owed me, and your dowry.

SUSANNA
Take this purse, too.

BARTOLO
And this as well.

FIGARO

Bravi, gittate pur, ch'io piglio ognora.

SUSANNA

Voliamo ad informar d'ogni avventura Madama e nostro zio. Chi al par di me contenta!

FIGARO

Io!

BARTOLO

Io!

MARCELLINA

Io!

SUSANNA, MARCELLINA, BARTOLO, FIGARO

E schiatti il signor Conte al gusto mio.

(all go out arm in arm. Enter Barbarina and Cherubino)

BARBARINA

Andiam, andiam, bel paggio, in casa mia tutte ritroverai le più belle ragazze del castello, di tutte sarai tu certo il più bello.

CHERUBINO

Ah! Se il Conte mi trova! Misero me! Tu sai che partito ei mi crede per Siviglia.

BARBARINA

Oh ve' che maraviglia! E se ti trova, non sarà cosa nuova. Odi! Vogliamo vestirti

FIGARO

Wonderful; throw them as long as I can catch them.

SUSANNA

I must go and tell Madame and my uncle of all that's happened; who is as happy as I am?

FIGARO

I am!

BARTOLO

I am!

MARCELLINA

I am!

SUSANNA, MARCELLINA, BARTOLO, FIGARO

Let the Count burst for my happiness!

BARBARINA

Come, come, handsome page, at my cottage you will find all the prettiest girls in the castle, and you will be the fairest of all.

CHERUBINO

Ah! If the Count should find me! Unhappy I! You know that he believes I've left for Seville.

BARBARINA

So what of it? If he finds you, that will be nothing new. Listen! I want to dress you

come noi, tutte insiem andrem poi a pre-
sentar de' fiori a Madamina. Fidati, o
Cherubin, di Barbarina.

like us, and all together we'll go to present
flowers to Madame. Have faith, O Cherubino, in Barbarina.

(they go out. The Countess enters)

disc no. 2/track 8 *No. 19: Recitative and Aria* But we are brought back, just as quickly
and just as potently to the more serious matter at hand: the Countess's unhappiness. This is an interior monologue—the Countess is thinking about how terri-
bly sad her situation has become, what she has had to accept—and she recalls,
in the aria (at 01:55) happier days, and she even wishes she were able to
expunge them from her memory. But (at 04:35), with an abrupt tempo change,
the aria takes a turn towards a ray of hope—the Countess realizes that if her
love is strong enough to survive, perhaps the Count's affections will return to
her. Here is the Countess in all her glory.

CONTESSA

E Susanna non vien! Sono ansiosa di saper
come il Conte accolse la proposta. Alquan-
to ardito il progetto mi par, e ad uno sposo
sì vivace e geloso! Ma che mal c'è? Can-
giando i miei vestiti con quelli de Susanna,
e i suoi coi miei a favor della notte. Oh
cielo! A qual'umil stato fatale io son ridotta
da un consorte crudel! Che dopo avermi
con un misto inaudito d'infedeltà, di
gelosia, di sdegno—prima amata, indi offe-
sa, e alfin tradita—fammi or cercar da una
mia serva aita! Dove sono i bei momenti di
dolcezza e di piacer, dove andaron i giura-
menti di quel labbro menzogner! Perché
mai, se in pianti e in pene per me tutto si
cangiò, la memoria di quel bene dal mio
sen non trapassò? Dove sono i bei momenti, ecc. Ah! Se almen la mia costanza nel

COUNTESS

Still Susanna does not come! I am anxious
to know how the Count received the pro-
posal. The scheme appears rather daring,
with a husband so forceful and jealous! But
what's the harm in it? Changing my clothes
for those of Susanna, and she for mine,
under cover of night. Heavens! To what
humble and dangerous state I am reduced
by a cruel husband, who, after having with
an unheard-of-combination of infidelity,
jealousy and disdain—having first loved
me, then abused and finally betrayed me—
now forces me to seek the help of a servant!
Where are the golden moments of tran-
quility and pleasure; what became of the
oaths of that deceitful tongue? Why did
not, when my life changed into tears and
pain, the memory of that joy disappear

languire amando ognor mi portasse una
speranza di cangiar l'ingrato cor. Ah! Se
almen la mia costanza, ecc.

from my breast? Where are the golden
moments, etc. Ah! If then my constancy
still loves through its sorrow, the hope yet
remains of changing that ungrateful heart.
Ah! If then my constancy, etc.

(she goes out. The Count comes in with Antonio)

Recitative

ANTONIO
Io vi dico signor, che Cherubino è ancora
nel castello, e vedete per prova il suo cappello.

ANTONIO
I tell you, sir, that Cherubino is still inside
the castle, and you can see his cap here as
proof.

CONTE
Ma come se a quest'ora esser giunto a
Siviglia egli dovria?

COUNT
But how can this be if he is already at
Seville?

ANTONIO
Scusate, oggi Siviglia è a casa mia. Là
vestissi da donna e là lasciati ha gl'altri abiti
suoi.

ANTONIO
Pardon, but today Seville is at my house;
he dressed as a woman there and left
behind some of his clothes.

CONTE
Perfidi!

COUNT
Villains!

ANTONIO
Andiam, e li vedrete voi.

ANTONIO
Come on, and you'll see for yourself.

(they go out. The Countess and Susanna come in)

CONTESSA
Cosa mi narri? E che ne disse il Conte?

COUNTESS
You don't say! And what was the Count's
answer?

SUSANNA
Gli si leggeva in fronte il dispetto e la rabbia.

CONTESSA
Piano, che meglio or lo porremo in gabbia!
Dov'è l'appuntamento, che tu gli proponesti?

SUSANNA
In giardino.

CONTESSA
Fissiamogli un loco. Scrivi.

SUSANNA
Ch'io scriva, ma, signora...

CONTESSA
Eh scrivi, dico, e tutto io prendo su me stessa.

SUSANNA
Anyone could see the spite and anger in his face.

COUNTESS
Keep your voice down, so we can get him in our trap. Where is the meeting you promised him supposed to take place?

SUSANNA
In the garden.

COUNTESS
Give him a definite place. Write to him.

SUSANNA
I would write, but, my lady...

COUNTESS
Come on and write, I say; I'll take the responsibility myself.

disc no. 2/track 10 *no 20: Duettino* Here the Countess and Susanna hatch the plot in its final form, and since the rendezvous is to take place in the garden, amid the pines and gentle breezes, the duettino is pastoral and quiet. The women are pleased with their own ingenuity and this moment of peace is a real joy.

(dictating)

Canzonetta sull'aria...

"A little tune on the breeze."

SUSANNA *(Scrivendo)*
Sull'aria...

SUSANNA *(writing)*
"On the breeze"

CONTESSA
Che soave zeffiretto—

COUNTESS
"What a gentle zephyr—

SUSANNA
Zeffiretto -

CONTESSA
questa sera spirerà -

SUSANNA
questa sera spirerà -

CONTESSA
sotto i pini del boschetto -

SUSANNA
sotto i pini?

CONTESSA
sotto i pini del boschetto -

SUSANNA
sotto i pini del boschetto -

CONTESSA
ei già il resto capirà,

SUSANNA
certo, certo il capirà.

CONTESSA
ei già il resto capirà.

CONTESSA
Canzonetto sull'aria, ecc.

SUSANNA
Che soave zeffiretto, ecc.

SUSANNA
zephyr –

COUNTESS
will sigh this evening –

SUSANNA
this evening" –

COUNTESS
beneath the pines in the thicket..."

SUSANNA
beneath the pines?

COUNTESS
"Beneath the pines in the thicket."

SUSANNA
"Beneath the pines in the thicket."

COUNTESS
He will understand the rest.

SUSANNA
Certainly, he'll understand.

COUNTESS
He will understand the rest.

COUNTESS
"Little tune on the breeze." etc.

SUSANNA
"What a gentle zephyr." etc.

Recitative

Piegato è il foglio; or come si sigilla?

I've folded the sheet, now how shall I seal it?

CONTESSA
Ecco... prendi una spilla, servirà di sigillo; attendi, scrivi sul riverso del foglio: rimandate il sigillo.

COUNTESS
Here, take a pin. It will serve as a seal. Wait: write on the back of the sheet. "Send back the seal."

SUSANNA
È più bizzarro di quel della patente.

SUSANNA
A cleverer stroke than the business of the commission.

CONTESSA
Presto nascondi: io sento venir gente.

COUNTESS
Quickly, hide; I hear someone coming.

(Susanna puts the letter in her bosom. Barbarina comes in with a group of peasant girls, and Cherubino also dressed like a peasant girl. They have bunches of flowers)

No. 21: Chorus

CORO
Ricevete, o padroncina queste rose e questi fior, che abbiam colte stamattina, per mostrarvi il nostro amor. Siamo tante contadine, e siam tutte poverine, ma quel poco che rechiamo ve lo diamo di buon cor.

CHORUS
Receive, beloved protectress, these roses and violets we gathered this morning to prove our love for you. We are only peasant girls and we are all poor, but what little we possess we give you with a good heart.

Recitative

BARBARINA
Queste sono, Madama, le ragazze del loco che il poco ch'han vi vengono ad offrire, e vi chiedon perdon del loro ardire.

BARBARINA
Madame, these girls are maids of the countryside; what little they have they offer you, and beg pardon for their presumption.

CONTESSA
Oh brave! Vi ringrazio.

COUNTESS
Wonderful! I thank you.

SUSANNA
Come sono vezzose.

SUSANNA
How pretty they are!

CONTESSA
E chi è, narratemi, quell'amabil fanciulla
ch'ha l'aria sì modesta?

(points to Cherubino)

BARBARINA
Ell' è una mia cugina e per le nozze è venuta ier sera.

CONTESSA
Onoriamo la bella forestiera; venite qui, datemi i vostri fiori. Come arrossì! Susanna, e non ti pare... che somigli ad alcuno?

SUSANNA
Al naturale...

(enter the Count and Antonio, who pulls off Cherubino's head-dress and plants his soldier's cap in its place)

ANTONIO
Eh cospettaccio! È questi l'uffiziale.

CONTESSA
Oh stelle!

SUSANNA
Malandrino.

CONTE
Ebben, Madama!

CONTESSA
Io sono, signor mio, irritata e sorpresa al par di voi.

COUNTESS
And tell me, who is that lovable girl with such a modest air?

BARBARINA
She is a cousin of mine, and arrived yesterday evening for the wedding.

COUNTESS
Let us honour the beautiful girl; come here and give me your flowers. How she blushed! Susanna, doesn't she seem to resemble someone?

SUSANNA
She certainly does.

ANTONIO
By God's Body! There's your officer.

COUNTESS
Heavens!

SUSANNA
Scoundrel.

COUNT
Well, Madame...

COUNTESS
My lord, I am as angry and surprised as you.

CONTE
Ma stamane?

CONTESSA
Stamane... per l'odierna festa volevam travestirlo al modo stesso che l'han vestito adesso.

CONTE
E perchè non partisti?

CHERUBINO
Signor...

CONTE
Saprò punire la tua disubbidienza.

BARBARINA
Eccellenza! Eccellenza! Voi mi dite sì spesso qualvolta m'abbracciate, e mi baciate: Barbarina, se m'ami, ti darò quel che brami...

CONTE
Io dissi questo?

BARBARINA
Voi! Or datemi, padrone, in sposo Cherubino, e v'amerò, com'amo il mio gattino.

CONTESSA
Ebbene, or tocca a voi.

ANTONIO
Brava figliuola! Hai buon maestro, che ti fa la scuola.

COUNT
But this morning?

COUNTESS
This morning...we planned to dress him for the day's festivity in the fashion in which he has dressed himself.

COUNT
And why did you not leave?

CHERUBINO
Sir...

COUNT
Your disobedience shall be punished.

BARBARINA
Your Excellency, Your Excellency! You told me yourself, that time when you hugged and kissed me, "Barbarina, if you'll love me, I'll give you whatever you want."

COUNT
I said that?

BARBARINA
You did. So, my lord, give me Cherubino as husband, and I'll love you as I love my kitten.

COUNTESS
Well, it's up to you.

ANTONIO
Well spoken, my daughter! You have been taught by a good teacher.

CONTE *(tra sé)*
Non so qual uom, qual demone, qual dio
rivolga tutto quanto a torto mio.

(enter Figaro)

FIGARO
Signor, se trattenete tutte queste ragazze,
addio feste, addio danza.

CONTE
E che? Vorresti ballar col piè stravolto?

FIGARO
Eh non mi duol più molto. Andiam belle
fanciulle.

CONTE
Per buona sorte i vasi eran di creta.

FIGARO
Senza fallo. Andiamo dunque, andiamo.

ANTONIO
E intanto a cavallo di galoppo a Siviglia
andava il paggio.

FIGARO
Di galoppo, o di passo, buon viaggio! Venite o belle giovani.

CONTE
E a te la sua patente era in tasca rimasta.

COUNT *(aside)*
I know not what man, what demon or god
has turned all these wrongs on me.

FIGARO
Sir, if you detain all of these girls then
goodbye to the feasting and dancing.

COUNT
What! Would you dance with a sprained
ankle?

FIGARO
Oh, it doesn't hurt much any longer. Come
on, pretty maidens.

COUNT
Lucky that the pots were made of clay.

FIGARO
How true. Well, come on, come on.

ANTONIO
And meanwhile the page was galloping
toward Seville.

FIGARO
At a gallop or a walk, prosperous journey!
Come, my fine girls.

COUNT
And his commission stayed behind inside
your pocket.

FIGARO
Certamente.
(Che razza di domande!)

ANTONIO (*a Susanna che fa dei moti a Figaro*)
Via, non gli far più moti, ei non t'intende.

(taking Cherubino by the hand and presenting him to Figaro)

Ed ecco chi pretende che sia un bugiardo il mio signor nipote.

FIGARO
Cherubino!

ANTONIO
Or ci sei.

FIGARO (*al Conte*)
Che diamin canta?

CONTE
Non canta, no, mia dice, ch'egli saltò stamane in sui garofani.

FIGARO
Ei lo dice! Sarà... se ho saltato io, si può dare ch'anch'esso abbia fatto lo stesso.

CONTE
Anch'esso?

FIGARO
Perché no? Io non impugno mai quel che non so.

FIGARO
Certainly.
(These are funny questions!)

ANTONIO (*to Susanna, who is making signs to Figaro*)
Hey, stop making signs, he doesn't understand you.

And here is the man who claims that my good nephew is a liar.

FIGARO
Cherubino!

ANTONIO
Now you know.

FIGARO (*to the Count*)
What the devil is his tune?

COUNT
No tune; he's saying that the boy jumped out on his carnations this morning.

FIGARO
So he says!...But perhaps...if I jumped he, too, could have done the same thing.

COUNT
He, too?

FIGARO
Why not? I never deny matters of which I know nothing.

(the wedding march begins)

Ecco la marcia, andiamo! Ai vostri posti, oh belle, ai vostri posti! Susanna dammi il braccio!	There's the march, let's go! To your posts, my beauties, to your posts. Susanna, give me your arm.

SUSANNA *(Figaro prende Susanna pel braccio)*
Eccolo.

SUSANNA *(giving her arm)*
Here it is.

(they all go out, leaving the Countess and the Count)

CONTE
Temerari!

COUNT
Shameless!

CONTESSA
Io son di ghiaccio!

COUNTESS
I feel made of ice!

CONTE
Contessa!

COUNT
Countess!

CONTESSA
Or non parliamo. Ecco qui le due nozze, riceverle dobbiam, alfin si tratta d'una vostra protetta. Seggiamo.

COUNTESS
Don't speak now. Here are the two couples; we must receive them. In the end the question involves your protégée. Let us be seated.

CONTE
Seggiamo. (E meditiam vendetta!)

COUNT
Let us be seated (and meditate on revenge).

(they sit. Enter hunters with guns slung over their shoulders. Village folk, peasant boys and girls. Two young girls carry in the bridal veil and hat of white feathers; two others the gloves and bunch of flowers. Figaro is with Marcellina. Other girls carry a similar hat for Susanna. Bartolo is with Susanna; he leads her to the Count. She kneels and receives from him the hat, etc. Figaro takes Marcellina to the Countess who performs a similar function)

DUO RAGAZZE

Amanti costanti, seguaci d'onor, cantate,
lodate sì saggio signor. A un dritto cedendo
che oltraggia, che offende, ei caste vi rende
ai vostri amator.

CORO

Cantiamo, lodiamo sì saggio signor!

TWO GIRLS

Faithful lovers, Zealous in honour, sing the
praises of such a wise master. Renouncing a
right that insults and offends, he renders
you spotless to your beloved.

CHORUS

Sing the praises of such a wise master!

*(while kneeling before the Count Susanna tugs at his robe and shows him a letter;
she raises her hand to her head and the Count under the pretence of adjusting her
hat takes the letter and hides it. Susanna pays her respects and rises. Figaro goes to
receive her. Fandango. Marcellina rises presently and Bartolo steps up to receive her
from the Countess.)*

CONTE *(cava il biglietto e fa l'atto d'un uom che
rimase punto al dito: lo scuote, lo preme, lo succhia
e vedendo il biglietto sigillato colla spilla dice, git-
tando la spilla a terra)*
Eh, la solita usanza, le donne ficcan gli aghi
in ogni loco… ah, capisco il gioco!

FIGARO *(a Susanna)*
Un biglietto amoroso che gli diè nel passar
qualche galante, ed era sigillato d'una
spilla, ond'egli si punse il dito, il Narciso or
la cerca, oh che stordito!

CONTE

Andate amici! E sia per questa sera disposto
l'apparato nuziale, colla più ricca pompa,
io vo' che sia magnifica la festa, e canti, e
fochi, e gran cena, e gran ballo; e ognuno
impari com'io tratto color che a me son
cari.

CORO

Amanti costanti, ecc.

COUNT *(takes out the letter and reacts as if he
has pricked his finger: shakes it, presses it, sucks it,
and seeing that the letter was sealed with a pin,
throws the pin on the floor, saying:)*
Hmm, as usual…women have pins sticking
out everywhere. Ah! Ah! I get the idea!

FIGARO *(to Susanna)*
That was a love letter that someone gave
him in passing, and it was sealed with a
pin, on which he hurt his finger. The Narcissus is looking for it. Oh, what foolishness!

COUNT

Come, my friends, and for this evening let
all the trappings of marriage be made ready
with richest magnificence. I want the feast
to be a grand one: songs, torches, a grand
feast and a ball. And all shall see how I
treat those who are dear to me.

CHORUS

Faithful lovers, etc.

Act 4

The castle garden

(There is an arbour to the right and one to the left. Night. Barbarina enters, searching for something on the ground)

No. 23. Cavatina

BARBARINA
L'ho perduta, me meschina! Ah chi sa dove
sarà? Non la trovo. L'ho perduta!
Meschinella! ecc. E mia cugina? E il
padron, cosa dirà?

BARBARINA
I have lost it, unhappy me! Ah, who knows
where it is? I cannot find it, I have lost it,
unhappy me, etc. And my cousin, and my
lord—what will he say?

(Figaro and Marcellina appear)

Recitative

FIGARO
Barbarina, cos'hai?

FIGARO
Barbarina, what's the matter?

BARBARINA
L'ho perduta, cugino.

BARBARINA
I have lost it, cousin.

FIGARO
Cosa?

FIGARO
What?

MARCELLINA
Cosa?

BARBARINA
La spilla, che a me diede il padrone per recar a Susanna.

FIGARO
A Susanna, la spilla? E così, tenerella, il mestiere già sai di far tutto sì ben quel che tu fai?

BARBARINA
Cos' è? Vai meco in collera?

FIGARO
E non vedi ch'io scherzo? Osserva:

(he takes a pin from Marcellina's dress)

questa è la spilla che il Conte da recare ti diede alla Susanna, e servia di sigillo a un bigliettino; vedi s'io sono istrutto.

BARBARINA
E perché il chiedi a me quando sai tutto?

FIGARO
Avea gusto d'udir come il padrone ti diè la commissione.

BARBARINA
Che miracoli! "Tieni, fanciulla, reca questa spilla alla bella Susanna, e dille: questo è il sigillo de' pini!"

FIGARO
Ah! Ah! De' pini.

MARCELLINA
What?

BARBARINA
The pin that His Lordship gave me to return to Susanna.

FIGARO
To Susanna? The pin? At such a tender age you already know how to ply your trade so well?

BARBARINA
What's the matter? Are you angry with me?

FIGARO
Don't you see I'm joking? Look:

this is the pin that the Count told you to return to Susanna, and it was used to seal a little letter. You see, I know all about it.

BARBARINA
Then why do you ask me if you know?

FIGARO
I wanted to hear how our patron gave you your instructions.

BARBARINA
It's funny! "Here, my girl, take this pin back to the beautiful Susanna, and tell her: this is the seal of the pines."

FIGARO
Ah, ah! Of the pines!

BARBARINA
È ver ch'ei mi soggiunse: guarda che alcun non veda; ma tu già tacerai.

FIGARO
Sicuramente.

BARBARINA
A te già niente preme.

FIGARO
Oh niente, niente.

BARBARINA
Addio, mio bel cugino; vo' da Susanna, e poi da Cherubino.

(she leaves hurriedly)

FIGARO
Madre!

MARCELLINA
Figlio!

FIGARO
Son morto!

MARCELLINA
Calmati, figlio mio!

FIGARO
Son morto, dico.

MARCELLINA
Flemma, flemma, e poi flemma: il fatto è serio, e pensar ci convien! Ma guarda un

BARBARINA
And then he warned me, "Be careful that no one sees it." But you won't tell.

FIGARO
Absolutely not.

BARBARINA
It's no concern of yours.

FIGARO
Oh, none at all.

BARBARINA
Goodbye, dear cousin, I'll go and find Susanna and then Cherubino.

FIGARO
Mother!

MARCELLINA
My son!

FIGARO
I am finished!

MARCELLINA
Calm yourself, my son.

FIGARO
I'm finished, I tell you!

MARCELLINA
Phlegm, phlegm; be calm. The matter is serious and bears consideration! But wait a

poco, che ancor non sai di chi si prenda giuoco.

FIGARO
Ah, quella spilla, o madre, è quella stessa che poc'anzi ei raccolse.

MARCELLINA
È ver, ma questo al più ti porge un dritto ai stare in guardia e vivere in sospetto; ma non sai se in effetto...

FIGARO
All'erta dunque! Il loco del congresso so dov'è stabilito.

MARCELLINA
Dove vai, figlio mio?

FIGARO
A vendicar tutt' i mariti. Addio!

(he goes out)

Recitative

BARBARINA
Nel padiglione a manca, ei così disse: è questo, è questo! E poi se non venisse?

(She rushes into the hunting-lodge on the left)

FIGARO
È Barbarina! Chi va là?

(Basilio and Bartolo appear with a group of peasants and servants)

while, you still don't know who's the object of the joke.

FIGARO
Ah, that "pin," mother, is the same one the Count lately renounced.

MARCELLINA
That's true, but at most this warrants keeping on your guard, and being suspicious; but you don't know for certain...

FIGARO
On guard, then! I know where they have agreed to meet.

MARCELLINA
Where are you going, my son?

FIGARO
To avenge all husbands. Farewell!

BARBARINA
In the left-hand lodge, he said: yes, this is it! What if he doesn't come!

FIGARO
That was Barbarina. Who goes there?

BASILIO
Son quelli che invitasti a venir.

BARTOLO
Che brutto ceffo! Sembri un cospirator!
Che diamin sono quegli infausti apparati?

FIGARO
Lo vedrete fra poco. In questo stesso loco
celebrerem la festa della mia sposa onesta e
del feudal signor.

BASILIO
Ah buono, buono, capisco come egli è.
Accordati si son senza di me.

FIGARO *(a truppo di contadini e servi)*
Voi da questi contorni non vi scostate, e a
un fischio mio correte tutti quanti.

(Figaro leaves with the peasants and servants)

(Figaro returns alone)

No. 26: Recitative and Aria Figaro here foolishly believes that Susanna is about to give in to the Count. He's anxious and hurt at first, but in the aria (01:35) he offers a warning, speaking directly to the men in the audience, during which he manages to work himself into a frenzy, singing as many words in a short space of time as he can. By the end, when he has said all he can about them, he sings "The rest I won't say, because everyone knows it already." And what is it that he won't say, that we all know?

FIGARO
Tutto è disposto: l'ora dovrebbe esser vici-
na; io sento gente... è dessa! Non è alcun;

BASILIO
Those whom you invited to come here.

BARTOLO
What a scowl! You look like a conspirator!
Why the devil all these strange preparations?

FIGARO
You will soon see. On this spot we celebrate the rites of my honourable wife and
the lord of the manor.

BASILIO
Ah, good, good, I begin to understand.
They have reached agreement without me.

FIGARO *(to the peasants and servants)*
Stay in the area and don't go far off. When
I give the signal, come running, all of you.

FIGARO
Everything is ready: the hour must be near,
I hear them coming; it's she; no it's no

buia è la notte... ed io comincio omai a fare il scimunito mestiere di marito... Ingrata! Nel momento della mia cerimonia ei godeva leggendo: e nel verderlo io rideva di me senza saperlo. Oh Susanna! Susanna! Quanta pena mi costi! Con quell'ingenua faccia, con quegli occhi innocenti, chi creduto l'avria? Ah! Che il fidarsi a donna, è ognor follia. Aprite un po' quegli occhi, uomini incauti e sciocchi, guardate queste femmine, guardate cosa son! Queste chiamate dee dagli ingannati sensi, a cui tributa incensi la debole ragion, ecc. Son streghe che incantano per farci penar, sirene che cantano per farci affogar, civette che allettano per trarci le piume, comete che brillano per toglierci il lume. Son rose spinose son volpi vezzose; son orse benigne, colombe maligne, maestre d'inganni, amiche d'affanni, che fingono, mentono, amore non senton, non senton pietà. No, no, no, no, no! Il resto nol dico, già ognuno lo sa. Aprite un po' quegli occhi, ecc.

one. The night is dark, and I'm already beginning to ply the foolish trade of cuckolded husband. Ungrateful! At the moment of my wedding ceremony he enjoyed her through a letter, and seeing him laughed at myself without knowing it. Oh, Susanna, Susanna, how many pains have you cost me! With that artless face, with those innocent eyes, who would have believed it! Ah, it's always madness to trust a woman! Open your eyes for a moment, rash and foolish men, look at these women, look at what they are. You call them goddesses, with your befuddled senses, and pay them tribute with your weakened minds. They are witches who work spells to make you miserable, sirens who sing to make you drown, screech-owls that lure you to pluck out your feathers, comets that flash to take away your light. They are thorny roses, cunning vixen, hugging bears, spiteful doves, masters of deceit, friends of trouble, who pretend, lie, feel no love, feel no pity, no, no, no, no no! The rest I won't, because everyone knows it already. Open your eyes for a moment, etc.

(he hides in the trees. Susanna and the Countess appear dressed in each other's clothes. After, Marcellina)

Recitative

SUSANNA
Signora! ella mi disse che Figaro verravi.

SUSANNA
Madame, she told me that Figaro would come here.

MARCELLINA
Anzi è venuto. Abbassa un po' la voce.

MARCELLINA
Truly, he's already here. Lower your voice a bit.

SUSANNA
Dunque un ci ascolta, e l'altro dee venir a cercarmi. Incominciam.

MARCELLINA
Io voglio qui celarmi.

(she enters the left-hand arbour)

SUSANNA
Madama, voi tremate. Avreste freddo?

CONTESSA
Parmi umida la notte; io mi ritiro.

FIGARO
Eccoci della crisi al grande istante.

SUSANNA
Io sotto queste piante, se Madama il permette, resto a prendere il fresco una mezz'ora.

FIGARO
Il fresco, il fresco!

CONTESSA
Restaci in buon'ora.

(she hides)

SUSANNA
Il birbo è in sentinella. Divertiamci anche noi, diamogli la mercè de' dubbi suoi.

SUSANNA
So one man eavesdrops and the other will come to look for me. Let's start.

MARCELLINA
I'll hide in here.

SUSANNA
Madame, you're trembling; are you cold?

COUNTESS
The night seems humid; I'll withdraw.

FIGARO
Here we are at the moment of crisis.

SUSANNA
Within this grove, if Madame permits it, I shall stay and take the fresh air for half an hour.

FIGARO
Fresh air, fresh air!

COUNTESS
Stay as long as you wish.

SUSANNA
The rogue is watching. I, too, shall have my little sport, I'll pay him for his suspicions.

No. 27: Recitative and Aria Oddly, since Susanna is the heroine of the opera, she has had no solos up to this point. There's irony in the text, because Susanna is supposedly punishing Figaro for his doubting her, but rarely has a lovelier, more sincere song been sung. In the simple recitative (track 19) Figaro might just believe that Susanna is waiting for another man, but for the fact that he is not as swept away by the aria (track 20), which is, essentially, an ode to the pleasures of love and nature. The orchestra comments: strings whisper smoothly, like the murmuring of the water and the gentle breeze, and the woodwinds supply the smile of the grass and cool feel of the grass beneath Susanna's feet. This aria is an island of joy—an extension of Susanna's duettino with the Countess in Act III, but more personal.

Giunse alfin il momento, che godrò senza affanno in braccio all'idol mio! Timide cure! Uscite dal mio petto, a turbar non venite il mio diletto! Oh come par che all'amoroso foco l'amenità del loco, la terra e il ciel risponda, come la notte i furti miei seconda! Deh vieni non tardar, o gioia bella, vieni ove amore per goder t'appella, finché non splende in ciel notturna face; finché l'aria è ancor bruna, e il mondo tace. Qui mormora il ruscel, qui scherza l'aura, che col dolce sussurro il cor restaura, qui ridono i fioretti e l'erba è fresca, ai piaceri d'amor qui tutto adesca. Vieni, ben mio, tra queste piante ascose. Vieni, vieni! Ti vo' la fronte incoronar di rose!

At last the moment is near when carefree I shall exult in the embrace of him I worship. Timid care, be banished from my heart, and come not to disturb my joy. Oh, how the beauties of this place, of heaven and earth, respond to the fire of my love. How night furthers my designs! Come now, delay not, lovely joy, come where love calls you to pleasure. The nocturnal torch shines not yet in heaven; the air is still murky, and the earth silent. Here the brook murmurs, the breezes play and with gentle sighing refresh the heart. Here the flowers are laughing, and the grass is cool; all things beckon to love's delights. Come, my soul, within this hidden grove. Come! I would crown your brow with roses!

(she hides in the trees on the opposite side from Figaro)

Recitative

FIGARO
Perfida! E in quella forma meco mentia? Non so s'io veglio, o dormo.

FIGARO
Deceiver! So you lied to me with such skill! I don't know whether I'm awake or sleeping.

CHERUBINO (*entrando*)
La la la la la la la lera! Io sento gente, entri-
amo ove entrò Barbarina. Oh, vedo qui
una donna.

CONTESSA
Ahimè, meschina!

CHERUBINO
M'inganno! A quel cappello che nell'ombra
vegg'io parmi Susanna.

CONTESSA
E se il Conte ora vien, sorte tiranna!

CHERUBINO
Pian pianin, le andrò più presso, tempo
perso non sarà.

CONTESSA
Ah, se il Conte arriva adesso qualche
imbroglio accaderà!

CHERUBINO
Susannetta! Non risponde, colla mano il
volto asconde, or la burlo in verità.

CONTESSA (*cercando di andarsene*)
Arditello, sfacciatello, ite presto via di qua,
ecc.

CHERUBINO
Smorfiosa, maliziosa, io già so perché sei
qua, ecc.

CHERUBINO (*entering*)
La la la la la la lera! I hear someone, so
I'll go in where Barbarina went. Oh, I see a
woman in there.

COUNTESS
Ah, miserable me!

CHERUBINO
I was deceived! In that cap under a shadow
it looks like Susanna.

COUNTESS
And if the Count comes now, cruel fate!

CHERUBINO
Softly now I'll come closer to you, we shall
not waste any time.

COUNTESS
Ah, if the Count comes along what a fight
there will be!

CHERUBINO
Dearest Susanna! She doesn't answer, but
hides her face with her hand; now I shall
really tease her.

COUNTESS (*trying to get away*)
Presumptuous, impudent boy, go away
from here immediately, etc.

CHERUBINO
Mincing, malicious woman, I already know
why you're here, etc.

CONTE *(da lontano)*
Ecco qui la mia Susanna!

SUSANNA, FIGARO
Ecco qui 'uccellatore!

CHERUBINO
Non far meco la tiranna!

SUSANNA, CONTE, FIGARO
Ah! Nel sen mi batte il core!

CONTESSA
Via partite, o chiamo gente!

SUSANNA, CONTE, FIGARO
Un'altr'uom con lei si sta;

CHERUBINO
Dammi un bacio, o non fai niente;

SUSANNA, CONTE, FIGARO
Alla voce, è quegli il paggio.

CONTESSA
Anche un bacio! Che coraggio!

CHERUBINO
E perché far io non posso quel che il Conte
ognor farà?

SUSANNA, CONTESSA, CONTE, FIGARO
Temerario!

CHERUBINO
Oh ve' che smorfie! Sai ch'io fui dietro il
sofa.

COUNT *(from a distance)*
That must be my Susanna!

SUSANNA, FIGARO
Here comes the fowler!

CHERUBINO
Don't try to play the tyrant with me!

SUSANNA, COUNT, FIGARO
Ah, my heart is pounding in my breast!

COUNTESS
Quickly, go, or I'll call for help!

SUSANNA, COUNT, FIGARO
There is another man with her.

CHERUBINO
Give me a kiss, or you'll do nothing.

SUSANNA, COUNT, FIGARO
By his voice, that must be the page.

COUNTESS
A kiss, you say! What temerity!

CHERUBINO
And why can't I do what the Count always
does?

SUSANNA, COUNTESS, COUNT, FIGARO
Rash boy!

CHERUBINO
Why make a face? You know that I was
behind the chair!

SUSANNA, CONTESSA, CONTE, FIGARO
Se il ribaldo ancor sta saldo, la faccenda
guasterà.

CHERUBINO *(le vuol dare un bacio)*
Prendi intanto!

(the Count steps between them and receives the kiss himself)

CONTESSA, POI CHERUBINO
O cielo! Il Conte!

(Cherubino runs to hide in the left-hand arbour)

FIGARO
Vo' veder cosa fan là.

(the Count makes a swipe at Cherubino but strikes Figaro instead)

CONTE
Perché voi non ripetete ricevete questo qua!

FIGARO, CONTESSA, CONTE, SUSANNA
Ah! Ci ho/ha fatto un bel guadagno colla
mia curiosità/sua temerità, ecc.

(Figaro and Susanna go off in opposite directions)

CONTE
Partito è alfin l'audace, accostati, ben mio!

CONTESSA
Giacché così vi piace, eccomi qui, signor.

SUSANNA, COUNTESS, COUNT, FIGARO
If the rake stays much longer he'll ruin
everything.

CHERUBINO *(trying to kiss the Countess)*
I'll take it anyway!

COUNTESS, THEN CHERUBINO
Heavens! The Count!

FIGARO
I want to see what they're doing.

COUNT
So that you won't repeat the offence, take
that!

FIGARO, COUNTESS, COUNT, SUSANNA
Ah, I have/he has made quite a gain
through my curiosity/his temerity, etc.

COUNT
At last the rogue has gone, come nearer, my
dearest.

COUNTESS
If it please you thus, here I am, sir.

FIGARO
Che compiacente femmina! Che sposa di buon cor!

CONTE
Porgimi la manina!

CONTESSA
Io ve la do.

CONTE
Carina!

FIGARO
Carina?

CONTE
Che dita tenerelle! Che delicata pelle! Mi pizzica, mi stuzzica, m'empie d'un nuovo ardor! ecc.

SUSANNA, CONTESSA, FIGARO
La cieca prevenzione delude la ragione inganna i sensi ognor, ecc.

CONTE
Oltre la dote, oh cara! ricevi anco un brillante che a te porge un amante in pegno del suo amor.

(he gives her a ring)

CONTESSA
Tutto Susanna piglia dal suo benefattor.

SUSANNA, CONTE, FIGARO
Va tutto a maraviglia, ma il meglio manca ancor.

FIGARO
What a complaisant woman! What a good-hearted wife!

COUNT
Give me your hand.

COUNTESS
I give it to you.

COUNT
Dearest!

FIGARO
Dearest?

COUNT
What dainty fingers! What delicate skin! I'm tingling, I'm feverish, I'm filled with new ardour, etc.

SUSANNA, COUNTESS, FIGARO
Blind precipitousness deludes reason and always tricks the senses, etc.

COUNT
Besides your dowry, beloved, receive this jewel, offered by a lover in pledge of his love.

COUNTESS
Susanna owes everything to her benefactor.

SUSANNA, COUNT, FIGARO
Everything is going perfectly! But the best is coming yet.

CONTESSA
Signor, d'accese fiaccole io veggio il balenar.

CONTE
Entriam, mia bella Venere, andiamoci a celar, ecc.

SUSANNA, FIGARO
Mariti scimuniti, venite ad imparar.

CONTESSA
Al buio, signor mio?

CONTE
È quello che vogl'io: tu sai che là per leggere, io non desio d'entrar.

FIGARO
La perfida lo seguita, è vano il dubitar.

SUSANNA, CONTESSA
I furbi sono in trappola, comincia ben l'affar.

CONTE
Chi passa?

FIGARO
Passa gente!

CONTESSA
È Figaro! Men vo!

CONTE
Andate, andate! Io poi verrò.

COUNTESS
Sir, I can see the light from bright torches.

COUNT
Let us enter, my fair Venus, let us go in and hide, etc.

SUSANNA, FIGARO
All you deceived husbands, come and learn your lessons.

COUNTESS
In the dark, my lord?

COUNT
It is my wish: you know that I don't want to go inside and read.

FIGARO
The betrayer is following him; doubts are foolish now.

SUSANNA, COUNTESS
The rogues are in the trap, the affair is beginning well.

COUNT
Who goes there?

FIGARO
None of your business!

COUNTESS
It's Figaro! I'm going!

COUNT
Go on. I'll find you soon.

(the Count disappears in the bushes. The Countess goes out to the right)

FIGARO
Tutto è tranquillo e placido, entrò la bella Venere: col vago Marte prendere, nuovo Vulcan del secolo, in rete la potrò.

SUSANNA *(imitando la voce della Contessa)*
Ehi, Figaro! Tacete!

FIGARO
Oh, questa è la Contessa. A tempo qui guingete, vedrete là voi stessa il Conte e la mia sposa. Di propria man la cosa toccar io vi farò.

SUSANNA *(dimenticando di cangiare la voce)*
Parlate un po' più basso: di qua non muovo il passo, ma vendicar mi vo'.

FIGARO
(Susanna!) Vendicarsi!

SUSANNA
Sì.

FIGARO
Come potria farsi? La volpe vuol sorprendermi, e secondarla vo', ecc.

SUSANNA
L'iniquo io vo' sorprendere, poi so quel che farò, ecc.

FIGARO *(con finta premura)*
Ah, se Madama il vuole!

FIGARO
All is peaceful and silent: The beautiful Venus has gone to the embrace of her fond Mars, but a modern Vulcan will soon have her in his net.

SUSANNA *(in a feigned voice)*
Hey, Figaro, keep your voice down!

FIGARO
Oh, there is the Countess. You come at a perfect moment to see for yourself the Count with my wife. You'll be able to touch them with your very own hand.

SUSANNA *(forgetting to alter her voice)*
Speak a little lower: from the spot I shall not move until I am avenged.

FIGARO
(Susanna!) Avenged?

SUSANNA
Yes.

FIGARO
How can that be done? The vixen is trying to catch me, and I'm going to help her, etc.

SUSANNA
I'm going to catch the villain, and I know how to go about it, etc.

FIGARO *(with comic affectation)*
Ah, if it please Madame!

SUSANNA
Su via, manco parole!

FIGARO
Ah, Madama!

SUSANNA
Su via, manco parole!

FIGARO
Eccomi a vostri piedi, ho pieno il cor di foco. Esaminate il loco, pensate al traditor!

SUSANNA
Come la man mi pizzica!

FIGARO
Come il polmon mi si altera!

SUSANNA
Che smania! Che furor! ecc.

FIGARO
Che smania! Che calor! ecc.

SUSANNA
E senz'alcun affetto?

FIGARO
Suppliscavi il rispetto. Non perdiam tempo invano; datemi un po' la mano...

SUSANNA *(dandogli uno schiaffo)*
Servitevi, signor.

SUSANNA
Get up, not a word!

FIGARO
Ah, Madame!

SUSANNA
Get up, not a word!

FIGARO
Here I am at your feet, with my heart full of fire. Look around you, and remember the betrayer!

SUSANNA
How my hand is itching!

FIGARO
I can hardly breathe!

SUSANNA
What madness! What fury! etc.

FIGARO
What madness! What fever! etc.

SUSANNA
But there is no affection between us?

FIGARO
Let respect be enough. We must not let time pass in vain, give me your hand a moment.

SUSANNA *(in her natural voice, boxing his ears)*
Help yourself, sir.

FIGARO
Che schiaffo!

SUSANNA
Che schiaffo! E questo, e ancora questo, e questo, e poi quest'altro.

FIGARO
Non batter così presto!

SUSANNA
E questo, signor scaltro, e questo, e poi quest'altro ancor.

FIGARO
Oh schiaffi graziosissimi. Oh, mio felice amor! ecc.

SUSANNA
Impara, impara, o perfido, a fare il seduttor, ecc.

FIGARO
Pace, pace, mio dolce tesoro: io conobbi la voce che adoro, e che impressa ognor serbo nel cor.

SUSANNA
La mia voce?

FIGARO
La voce che adoro.

SUSANNA, FIGARO
Pace, pace, mio dolce tesoro! pace, pace, mio tenero amor.

FIGARO
You slapped me!

SUSANNA
You slapped me! Here's another, and another and still another.

FIGARO
Don't beat me so furiously!

SUSANNA
And another, you sharper, and then still one more!

FIGARO
Oh, most gracious blows! Oh, perfect love! etc.

SUSANNA
I'll teach you, deceitful man, to play the seducer, etc.

FIGARO
Peace, peace, my sweet treasure: I recognised the voice which I adore and carry engraved in my heart.

SUSANNA
My voice?

FIGARO
The voice I adore.

SUSANNA, FIGARO
Peace, peace, my sweet treasure, peace, peace, my gentle beloved.

(the Count returns)

CONTE
Non la trovo, e girai tutto il bosco.

SUSANNA, FIGARO
Questi è il Conte, alla voce il conosco.

CONTE
Ehi, Susanna! Sei sorda, sei muta?

SUSANNA
Bella, bella! Non l'ha conosciuta!

FIGARO
Chi?

SUSANNA
Madama.

FIGARO
Madama?

SUSANNA
Madama!

SUSANNA, FIGARO
La commedia, idol mio, terminiamo, consoliamo il bizzaro amator, ecc.

(Figaro throws himself at her feet)

FIGARO
Sì, Madama, vio siete il ben mio.

CONTE
La mia sposa! Ah, senz arme son io!

COUNT
I cannot find her, and I've combed the forest.

SUSANNA, FIGARO
That's the Count, I recognise his voice.

COUNT
Hey, Susanna, are you deaf or dumb?

SUSANNA
Wonderful! He didn't recognise her!

FIGARO
Whom?

SUSANNA
Madame.

FIGARO
Madame?

SUSANNA
Madame!

SUSANNA, FIGARO
Let's terminate this farce, my beloved, and console this capricious lover, etc.

FIGARO
Yes, Madame, you are the light of my life.

COUNT
My wife? Ah, I have no weapons!

FIGARO
Un ristoro al mio cor concedete?

SUSANNA
Io son qui fate quel che volete.

CONTE
Ah, ribaldi, ribaldi!

SUSANNA, FIGARO
Ah, corriamo, corriamo mio bene e le pene
compensi il piacer.

FIGARO
Will you grant a cure for my heart?

SUSANNA
Here I am, I'll do as you wish.

COUNT
Ah, scandalous, scandalous!

SUSANNA, FIGARO
Ah, let us make haste, beloved, and
exchange pain for pleasure.

(they move towards the arbour on the left. The Count grasps Figaro)

disc no. 2/track 26 After fifteen minutes of confusion, face-slapping, humiliation, playfulness and not-so-playfulness, and the loving reconciliation of Susanna and Figaro, the Count, in all his mania, takes over, making one mistake after another, and refusing to pardon the wrongdoers. But when the Countess reveals herself (01:06) it is left only for the Count to apologize to her (01:30). He does so with such simplicity and beauty that the Countess melts at once, commenting that she is kinder than he, and so forgives more easily. Everyone is exhausted after this day of intense plotting and turmoil and joins in a quick chorus (04:10) in which they all agree to celebrate what appears like the restoration of order, as the curtain falls.

CONTE
Gente, gente, all'armi, all'armi!

FIGARO *(con finto spavento)*
Il padrone!

CONTE
Gente, gente, aiuto, aiuto!

COUNT
Help, help, weapons, weapons!

FIGARO *(feigning great fright)*
The master!

COUNT
My men, help, help!

(enter Antonio, Basilio, Bartolo, Don Curzio and servants)

FIGARO
Son perduto!

BASILIO, CURZIO, ANTONIO, BARTOLO
Cos'avvenne? Cos'avvenne?

CONTE
Il scellerato m'ha tradito, m'ha infamato, e con chi state a veder.

BASILIO, CURZIO, ANTONIO, BARTOLO
Son stordito, sbalordito, non mi par che ciò sia ver!

FIGARO
Son storditi, sbalorditi, oh che scena, che piacer!

(going to the arbour the Count hands out, in turn, Cherubino, Barbarina, Marcellina and Susanna)

CONTE
Invan resistete, uscite, Madama; il premio ora avrete di vostra onestà ... Il paggio!

ANTONIO
Mia figlia!

FIGARO
Mia madre!

BASILIO, CURZIO, ANTONIO, BARTOLO
Madama!

CONTE
Scoperta è la trama la perfida è qua!

FIGARO
I'm lost!

BASILIO, CURZIO, ANTONIO, BARTOLO
What happened?

COUNT
The villain has betrayed me, has defamed me, and you shall see with whom.

BASILIO, CURZIO, ANTONIO, BARTOLO
I'm amazed, confounded, I can't believe it's true!

FIGARO
They're amazed, confounded, oh, what a scene, what fun!

COUNT
In vain you resist, come out Madame; now you shall be rewarded for your honesty... The page!

ANTONIO
My daughter!

FIGARO
My mother!

BASILIO, CURZIO, ANTONIO, BARTOLO
Madame!

COUNT
The plot is revealed, and there is the deceiver.

SUSANNA *(inginocchiandosi)*
Perdono, perdono!

CONTE
No, no! Non sperarlo!

FIGARO *(inginocchiandosi)*
Perdono, perdono!

CONTE
No, no, non vo' darlo!

TUTTI SLAVO IL CONTE *(inginocchiandosi)*
Perdono! ecc.

CONTE
No!

(the Countess emerges from the right-hand arbour)

CONTESSA
Almeno io per loro perdono otterrò.

BASILIO, CURZIO, CONTE, ANTONIO, BARTOLO
Oh cielo! Che veggio! Deliro! Vaneggio!
Che creder non so.

CONTE *(inginocchiandosi)*
Contessa perdono! Perdono, perdono!

CONTESSA
Più docile io sono, e dico di sì.

TUTTI
Ah! Tutti contenti saremo così. Questo
giorno di tormenti, di capricci e di follia, in

SUSANNA *(kneeling)*
Pardon, pardon.

COUNT
No, no, do not expect it!

FIGARO *(kneeling)*
Pardon, pardon!

COUNT
No, no, I will not!

ALL EXCEPT THE COUNT *(kneeling)*
Pardon! etc.

COUNT
No!

COUNTESS
At least I may obtain their pardon.

BASILIO, CURZIO, COUNT, ANTONIO, BARTOLO
Heaven! What do I see? I'm raving! Going
crazy! I don't know what to believe.

COUNT *(kneeling)*
Countess, your pardon! Pardon!

COUNTESS
I am more clement, and answer, yes.

ALL
Ah! All shall be made happy thereby. Only
love can resolve this day of torments,

contenti e in allegria solo amor può termi-
nar. Sposi, amici, al ballo, al gioco, alle
mine date foco! Ed a suon di lieta marcia
corriam tutti a festeggiar, ecc.

caprice and folly, into joy and happiness.
Spouses and sweethearts, to dancing and
fun, and let's have some fireworks! And to
the sound of a gay march hurry off to celebrate, etc.

END OF THE OPERA

The Marriage of Figaro

WOLFGANG AMADEUS MOZART

COMPACT DISC ONE 76:46:00

Overture   4:21
Act One

[1] Cinque, dieci, venti   2:48
     Figaro/Susanna
[2] Se a caso Madama   2.28
     Figaro/Susanna
[3] Bravo, signor padrone—Se vuol ballare   3.18
     Figaro
[4] La vendetta, oh, la vendetta   3.10
     Bartolo
[5] Via, resti servita   2.16
     Susanna/Marcellina
[6] Non so più cosa son, cosa faccio   2.35
     Cherubino
[7] Cosa sento!   4.45
     Count/Basilio/Susanna
[8] Non più andrai farfallone amoroso   3.35
     Figaro

Act Two

[9]   Porgi amor   4.15
      Countess
[10] Vieni, cara Susanna   4.17
      Countess/Susanna/Cherubino

11	Voi, che sapete *Cherubino*	2.46
12	Bravo! Che bella voce! *Countess/Susanna/Cherubino*	1.03
13	Venite, inginocchiatevi *Susanna*	3.20
14	Quante buffonerie! *Countess/Susanna/Cherubino/Count*	3.24
15	Susanna, or via sortite *Count/Countess/Susanna*	3.09
16	Dunque voi non aprite? *Count/Countess*	0.52
17	Aprite, presto, aprite *Susanna/Cherubino*	0.57
18	Oh guarda il demonietto *Susanna/Count/Countess*	1.39
19	Esci ormai, garzon mainato *Count/Countess*	2.44
20	Susanna! Susanna! *Count/Countess/Susanna*	5.26
21	Signori, di fuori! *Figaro/Count/Susanna/Countess*	3.30
22	Ah! Signor, signor! *Antonio/Count/Susanna/Countess/Figaro*	6.03
23	Voi Signor, che giusto siete *Marcellina/Basilio/Bartolo/Susanna/Countess/Figaro/Count*	3.54

COMPACT DISC TWO   78.02

Act Three

1	Che imbarazzo è mai questo *Count/Countess/Susanna*	2.17
2	Crudel! Perche finora farmi languir così? *Count/Susanna*	2.44
3	E perchè fosti meco	0.41

Count/Susanna/Figaro

4 Hai già vinta la causa— Vedrò mentr'io sospiro   4.51
Count

5 E decisa la lite   1.46
Don Curzio/Marcellina/Figaro/Count/Bartolo

6 Riconosci in questíamplesso   4.56
Marcellino/Figaro/Bartolo/Don Curzio/Count/Susanna

7 Eccovi, o caro amico   1.47
Marcellina/Bartolo/Susanna/Figaro/Barbarina/Cherubino

8 E Susanna non vien!...Dove sono   6.22
Countess

9 Io vi dico, signor   0.52
Antonio/Count/Countess/Susanna

10 Canzonetta sull'aria...   3.06
Countess/Susanna

11 Ricevete, o padroncina   4.00
Chorus/Barbarina/Countess/Susanna/Antonio/Count/Cherubino/Figaro

12 Ecco la marcia   6.44
Figaro/Susanna/Count/Countess/Young men/Chorus

Act Four

13 L'ho perduta, me meschina!   1.50
Barbarina

14 Barbarina, cos'hai?   2.10
Figaro/Barbarina/Marcellina

15 Nel padiglione a manca   1.13
Barbarina/Figaro/Basilio/Bartolo

16 Ha I diavoli nel corpo!...In quegli anni   4.37
Basilio/Bartolo

17 Tutto è disposto... Aprite un po'quegli occhi   4.22
Figaro

18 Signora, ella mi disse...   0.44
Susanna/Marcellina/Countess/Figaro

19 Giunse alfin il momento   1.17
Susanna

20	Deh vieni, non tardar	3.19
	Susanna	
21	Perfida! E in quella forma meco mentia?	0.34
	Figaro/Cherubino/Countess	
22	Pian, pianin...	3.24
	Cherubino/Countess/Count/Susanna/Figaro	
23	Partito è alfin l'audace	2.46
	Count/Countess/Figaro/Susanna	
24	Tutto è tranquillo e placido	4.05
	Figaro/Susanna	
25	Pace, pace mio dolce tesoro	2.09
	Figaro/Susanna/Count	
26	Ecco la marcia	5.17
	All	

PHOTOGRAPHY CREDITS

Archive Photos: pgs. 12, 16, 28, 32
Austrian National Tourist Office: p: 14
Jack Vartoogian: pgs. 18, 22, 31, 35
New York Public Library: pgs. 21, 24, 36
Bridgeman Art Library: pgs. 27/Mozart Museum, Vienna,
33/Roger-Viollet, Paris
Culver Pictures: p. 45
Beth Bergman: pgs. 47, 48
Stills: p. 49/Lebedinsky

Cover Image: National Gallery, Budapest, Hungary/ET Archive,
London/SuperStock